Ordinary
Miracles

Ordinary Miracles

True Stories of an Extraordinary God
Who Works in Our Everyday Lives

Rebekah Montgomery

PROMISE
PRESS
An Imprint of Barbour Publishing

Many of the names in this book have been changed
to protect the individuals
from embarrassment or danger.

ISBN 1-57748-744-3

Unless otherwise noted, scripture quotations are taken from the
King James Version of the Bible.

Scriptures marked NIV are taken from the HOLY BIBLE: New
International Version®. NIV®. Copyright © 1973, 1978, 1984 by
International Bible Society. Used by permission of Zondervan
Publishing House.

Published by Promise Press, an imprint of Barbour Publishing,
Inc., P.O. Box 719, Uhrichsville, Ohio 44683
http://www.barbourbooks.com

 Member of the
Evangelical Christian
Publishers Association

Printed in the United States of America.

I am convinced that miracles occur far more often than most people know or recognize. Not all of them are experienced by Christian believers; a fair number are given to people who are downright rapscallions and heathens. But all of them come from a God who remembers that He made us out of dirt, loves us earthly folks, and knows we need His help—and lots of it.

Daily, all over the globe, Christian believers and people in need ask God to intervene in their lives. And He does! It happens so often that many consider it an ordinary, everyday experience. An ordinary miracle, if you will. They ask. He answers. And like nine out of ten lepers, they forget to thank Him or share their experiences with others.

The stories in this book are from a group of tenth lepers who have shared their spiritual adventures—and want to thank God.

Their gratitude and experiences are here to be shared, with devout believers, dyed-in-the-wool infidels, and all of those in between. Miracles encourage faith in God. They prompt people to think, "If God will do something miraculous for that rather commonplace person, maybe He will help me, too."

And He will.

For many Christian believers, miracles are such a

daily experience that they downgrade them to the "answers to prayer" category instead. They may consider miracles to be only those extraordinary experiences where lightning flashes across the sky, thunder rolls, and the voice of God audibly says, "Pay attention! I'm going to do more than you ask or think here!"

Or they may be embarrassed to admit that they were in such a seriously troubled situation that it took a miracle from God to bail them out.

Or they may fear someone will brand them as a religious extremist if they claim God worked a miracle in their lives.

However, every time God breaks into our lives and supplies a need, arranges a circumstance, or sends help out of nowhere, those are miracles as surely as when the dying child is restored to health, the barren woman conceives, and five thousand hungry people are fed fish sandwiches from a kid's snack.

Also, some people, even Christian believers or religious folks, do not recognize miracles when they see them. They are like the bystanders who watched John baptize Christ, saw the dove descend, and heard the voice of God say, "This is my beloved Son," and thought, *Oh! It thundered!* They missed the moment, perhaps because they didn't expect—or didn't want—God to do anything supernatural. They would rather He stayed up in heaven on His own turf and didn't muck around on theirs. It messes up their tidy little world and makes them ask uncomfortable questions. One wonders if they would accept that a miracle was taking place before their very eyes if a neon sign were dropped from the heavens flashing on and off: "Miracle in Progress!"

It also rather surprised me to see that miracles do not always change the minds and lives of the people who witness them. They may recognize an event in their lives as a miracle from God, but they still remain resistant to surrendering their lives to Him. Like Judas who witnessed Jesus restore the dead to life, they still have fatal doubts. I'm not sure what they're waiting for. Perhaps for God to reinvent Himself in such a way as to be more acceptable to them, not quite so demanding. But their resistance does not negate the miracle.

I am further convinced that God performs a lot less miracles than He wants to. Many people simply don't ask God to bare His powerful arm on their behalf. I suspect that with His penchant for doing good things for His children and His love of surprising them with good gifts, He's disappointed when they don't ask.

I don't have a pat explanation as to why God performs miracles in some situations but not in others. I have seen some saints die horrible, wasting deaths while certified sinners are miraculously healed—and I've wondered at the seeming unfairness of it. I have also witnessed people who believe that God does perform miracles and have even been a conduit used by God to bring a miracle to someone else, and yet they go without one when they ask for divine intervention.

The Apostle Paul was one of those individuals. He believed in God's miraculous power. God used him to perform healings and even a resurrection or two. But when he asked for healing for his "thorn in the flesh," God said, "My grace is sufficient"—which can be translated: "You need this problem. It forces you to rely on Me."

And that, perhaps, is a partial answer to the why and why not for miracles.

If you're reading this book expecting to see stories about statues that bleed or signs of the stigmata, this is the wrong book for you. I don't know anything about those things, and I don't find any biblical examples of them. All of the stories you will read in this volume have a counterpart in Scripture. Someone mentioned in the Bible experienced something similar.

Even then, people doubt that miracles happen. But take note: The twentieth and twenty-first centuries have not been marked by God's dotage. He is still active and competent.

Despite rampant disbelief, incredulity, simple doubts, and folks hiding miracles under bushels, word of them still leaks out. They're poorly kept secrets. Of course they don't prove or disprove God. They only confirm what the Bible states: God loves sinful humanity. And He sent His Son to prove it. That is the most extraordinary miracle of all. For God, everything else He does is an ordinary miracle.

*O*n more than one occasion, God used the announcement of a pregnancy to certify that His word was true. He was going to do something supernatural in someone's life, and the news that a baby was coming was offered as proof.

Sarah was told she would bear a son as evidence that God would make a great nation from her and Abraham's descendants (Gen. 17:15, 18:10–15). Through an angel, God told Mary that her aged, formerly barren cousin Elizabeth was expecting a child. This was offered as proof that with the power of God, even Mary herself, a virgin, could conceive (Luke 1:34–36).

For the Miller family, God's message that Jenny was expecting a child bore proof that He was going to provide healing to their gravely ill little girl.

Anna's Cure

Early Autumn 1994

As a mother, Jenny Miller couldn't quiet the nagging feeling that something was very seriously wrong with three-year-old Anna, the next to the youngest of her five children.

"I had taken her to the pediatrician several times, and each time he said she was fine. But it wasn't just her thin arms that made me think she was sick," said Jenny. "When I would give her a piece of candy, she wouldn't eat it. She'd put it in her pocket, and I knew there was something wrong with that!"

October 13, 1994

As evening fell, Jenny attempted to stifle her fears for Anna.

Earlier that day, Jenny had again taken Anna to the

pediatrician. He had looked at her distended abdomen and skinny arms, but once more he pronounced her healthy. He thought that perhaps she might have a kidney infection or bronchitis.

But Anna was so weak she could barely walk. Her stomach didn't seem merely pudgy to Jenny, it seemed swollen; and Anna was coughing so hard she had trouble catching her breath. Jenny wondered if the child would live through the night.

In desperation, Jenny took Anna to the home of a physician friend from their church. When he examined the gravely ill child, he shared Jenny's concern.

"As a doctor, I can't tell you that your pediatrician is all wrong," he said cautiously, unwilling to criticize another physician. Then he gave Jenny the name of a different doctor and urged her to take Anna to see him in the morning.

The remainder of the evening was a nightmare for both mother and daughter.

"I propped Anna up on the couch, but she could hardly breathe. I saw fear in her eyes," said Jenny. That fear matched the terror in Jenny's own heart.

The next afternoon, the new doctor temporarily put Jenny's mind at ease. However, he admitted Anna to the university hospital for tests and observation. Jenny went home to care for her other children while her husband, J.P., stayed by Anna's side.

By 10 P.M., their newfound confidence was severely shaken by the results of a CAT scan.

"It might be cancer," J.P. told Jenny over the phone. "They've put chest tubes in because she is drowning in fluid."

As quickly as she could, Jenny drove back to the hospital. Attached to all kinds of tubes and machinery, Anna looked small and pale and vulnerable.

"I wanted to scoop her up and run out of the hospital," Jenny said later, but she knew she could not shield her beloved child from an uncertain future or protect her from the terrible disease that lurked inside her tiny body.

Jenny and J.P. held one another and prayed for their small daughter. "God, Anna is Yours. You can heal her or You can take her home. You know what is best."

"At that moment," said Jenny later, "I realized that she was in God's arms—and anything was possible with God."

Over the next weeks God continually gave Jenny confirmation that He was holding Anna in his arms. Card after card came with Isaiah 40:11 on it: "He tends his flock like a shepherd: He gathers the lambs in his arms and carries them close to his heart; he gently leads those that have young" (NIV).

Still, that night was very dark for Jenny. Uncertain what diagnosis tomorrow would bring, she and J.P. went home to their other children and spent a sleepless night.

Jenny lay in bed dreading the dawn, and when it finally came, she told J.P., "It's so hard to face today. I want to just stay in bed."

J.P. quietly told her, "Anna has to face the day."

"It put everything back into perspective for me," Jenny said. "I thought, *This might be hard for me, but it will really be hard for Anna.*"

Worse moments were yet to come.

Back at the hospital that morning, Jenny and J.P. sat down with the doctors who told them the awful truth: Anna had stage four of a form of cancer called *neuroblastoma*. Her tumor was the largest of this type that the hospital doctors had ever seen and was very progressed.

"What is beyond stage four?" Jenny asked.

The doctor was brutally honest. "Death," he said. "She has less than a 5 percent chance of survival." However, the doctor outlined a rigorous regime of chemotherapy and radiation.

Knowing how difficult chemotherapy could be, J.P. asked, "Is this prolonging something that's going to happen anyway? Is there a light at the end of the tunnel?"

"There is a light," said the doctor, "but it's a very small light and it's very far away."

As long as there was a chance, Jenny and J.P. decided not to give up. "We'll go ahead with the treatment plan and see what happens," they told the doctor.

Although she was in the intensive care unit for the

next six weeks, Anna immediately started radiation and the first of eight courses of chemotherapy. After that, she was in and out of the hospital so much that the Millers' four other children—all home-schooled—went intermittently to stay with their grandparents in Indiana.

March 1995

It was a quiet time at the Miller house, too quiet for Jenny. Her other children were with their grandparents and only a gravely ill Anna was in the house.

"I had been praying that God would give us some hope for the future," said Jenny. "I was praying that life could get back to normal." But even Jenny was surprised how God supplied that hope.

While she was holding Anna on the couch, Anna said to her, "Mom, you got a baby in your tummy."

Jenny and J.P. were shocked at the child's matter-of-fact announcement.

"How do you know?" they asked Anna.

"God told me," said Anna. "He stood by my bed in the hospital and said, 'Your mommy's got a baby in her tummy.'"

Although Jenny had no suspicions that she was pregnant, the next day she conducted a home pregnancy test. It was positive.

Jenny was apprehensive.

"I was anxious about having a new baby on top of my

responsibilities for Anna and the other kids," she said.

But shortly thereafter, J.P. and Anna were looking at a Bible picture book together.

"Daddy, that's what I saw!" Anna pointed at a picture of Christ. "Jesus in the sun! He said, 'Don't be afraid. You not gonna die!'"

Jenny said she then realized God had given comforting knowledge to Anna—and He had sent a message for her, as well.

"I had a peace that this was a sign from God. It was as if He was saying, 'You don't have to worry about November when the baby is due. Everything is going to be okay.'"

There was a great outpouring of love and prayers for Anna and the entire Miller family. "People at the grocery store would tell me that they were praying for Anna every day," said Jenny.

Then in June 1995, with a flood of prayer support, Anna had a stem cell transplant. She recovered and was able to go home in only three weeks' time, a record for a transplant recovery.

Anna began to regain her strength with amazing speed. She did well until October 1995. Two weeks before Jenny was due to deliver the new baby, Anna was stricken with shingles, a typical malady for a stem cell transplant patient. But she made a complete recovery, although her eyes remained sensitive to light. This was the last time Anna was hospitalized.

Jenny's son, Avery, was born November 6, 1995.

Postscript

Anna's life is a witness to the healing power of Christ. As a result of Anna's illness, combined with the witness of other believers, the doctor who diagnosed Anna's cancer came to commit his life to Christ.

At Anna's last follow-up CAT scan in December 1998, Jenny overheard a substitute doctor handling Anna's treatment remark to one of the nurses, "Boy, she is a real miracle! It's a miracle that she made it!"

Anna has had no reoccurrence of the cancer. If this continues, she will be considered cancer-free in another year.

Anna remembers little of her ordeal, but she has remained friendly with many of the nurses.

The Millers live in Columbia, Missouri, where J.P. owns a pest control company. Jenny still home-schools her children, and they've had another recent addition to the family, a new baby girl, which brings the number of their children to seven.

To give when you have needs yourself flies in the face of all human logic. Yet "Give, and it shall be given unto you" (Luke 6:38) is one of God's oddest but most miraculous principles. People who give generously to God will find themselves scooping up handfuls of blessings.

In the midst of a terrible drought, God called a widow with a son to make a tortilla of sorts for the prophet Elijah from the last supplies in her meager larder. When she obeyed, God miraculously multiplied her supplies until the drought ended (1 Kings 17:7–16).

In a similar way, a small church in Indiana found that it is still true that you can't outgive God.

BUILT ON A STRONG FOUNDATION

Mt. Hope Church of the Nazarene
Berne, Indiana

Some thought it was foolish for the Mt. Hope Church of the Nazarene to plan a work-and-witness trip to Caguas, Puerto Rico. They were in the middle of their own building program. Why traipse clear to Puerto Rico to build a worship center for someone else? Why not leave that job to bigger churches with more members—and more money?

Luanne and Merlin Frank, both longtime Christian believers, strongly felt that God had made an opportunity for them to take a construction team to build a church building in a densely populated area where a struggling group of believers were meeting in a semi-trailer. In spite of what seemed to be a conflict of time and money with their own church expansion program, they planned the trip and raised the money. Forty-four people from Mt. Hope Church signed on to go, each with different skills.

Wednesday, December 24, 1997
Two days before their flight, everything was ready—or so they thought. Months of praying, planning, packing, and anticipation culminated as the work team made final preparations for their Friday morning flight to Puerto Rico. Then, one of the team members suddenly had to drop out.

The elimination of a team member seemed opportune for Corey, the first person on the standby list. This teenage boy had really wanted to go, but the group had been unable to purchase a ticket for him. They thought it would be a simple matter to change the name on the ticket so Corey could go to Puerto Rico, too.

"No, it cannot be changed," the airline told them. "Not even if a penalty were paid."

A lot of praying went on through the night and over the next day.

"Several of us asked God for a miracle," Luanne remembers. "We reminded God that He had brought us this far. We had tried everything we knew to try to work it out ourselves, but to no avail. Only He could change the circumstances."

But just as God had worked out the financial plans for the trip a year before, He proved He was still in control now.

Friday Morning, December 26, 1997
As the bus taking the work team to the airport idled in the church parking lot, a member made one last-minute desperate call to the airlines. Nothing had worked before, and it was almost too late, but the call was made anyway.

This time, the call revealed some amazing information: The airline issues one free ticket for every twenty-nine paying passengers. The travel agency randomly chose a name to put on this free ticket. It was the name of the person who was now unable to go. Issued directly from the airline instead of the travel agency, it was the only ticket that could be changed!

"Words cannot express what happened inside each of us when we realized what had just taken place," said Luanne. "Amidst tears of joy and amazement, all forty-four of us boarded the bus, realizing that miracles didn't only happen in Bible times, they still happen today!"

But the story doesn't end there. Corey's addition to the work team was not an accident. While he was in Puerto Rico, Corey was part of a group of four individuals who befriended a nearby family of ten. "Corey is a teenager and the family had teenagers, so I believe God used him as a link in the chain that led them to the Lord," said Luanne.

Postscript

The bids for the new church construction were twice as high as first projected. However, after the church's decision to send a work team to Puerto Rico, a building contractor "fell in our laps," said Luanne, "and things started falling into place. We built the building at a much lower cost than expected."

Further: "On November 22, 1998, our new building was dedicated. On that Thanksgiving Sunday, we received an offering for world evangelization that exceeded our goal, the highest ever in the history of the church! Thank the Lord!"

Luanne is a homemaker and Merlin is now a maintenance man in a print shop, after retiring from twenty-six years of farming. The Franks have six children.

*D*eliverance is a strong theme in the Bible, another opportunity for God to show His miraculous power and love to His children.

The Israelites discovered this when they were caught in a squeeze play between the well-trained and well-armed Egyptian army and the unforgiving Red Sea.

Where could they go for safety? Through the waters on a dry path, protected by the hand of God (Exod. 14).

Young George Wallace Weiman was caught in the maelstrom that was the South Pacific during World War II. Trapped between the Imperial Japanese Army and the South Sea, God once again made a safe way through treacherous waters.

THE BULLETPROOF CLOAK

In late October 1942, young Marine Private George Wallace Weiman found himself alone in a foxhole on Guadalcanal.

Fresh out of boot camp, he had been on this, the largest of the British Solomon Islands, for only two days when he was marched to the front lines to join the first offensive against the Imperial Japanese Army. The battle had been raging since August 7. With bullets whizzing around him, Wallace dug a hole in the ground, climbed in it, and waited to either kill or be killed. He was to spend a lot of time in that hole.

"In the tropics," said Wallace, "the night comes suddenly. It gets very dark and you can't see your hand in front of your face. I could hear the Japanese moving through the night around me, but I couldn't see them."

Occasionally, Wallace heard a cry of discovery when enemy soldiers stumbled across a GI in a foxhole. Then would come the burst of machine-gun fire accompanied by flashes of light, the thud of bullets striking living flesh, and the scream of pain as a soul was wrenched from the body of a man and hurled into eternity. When daylight finally returned to the battlefield, it would reveal a participant of the midnight drama, slumped to the ground, frozen in his final bow.

As the battle continued, Wallace's days were filled with the struggle to survive the dangers of jungle warfare while at the same time fighting malaria, dysentery, poisonous reptiles, and exhaustion. Alone in a foxhole surrounded by the enemy, amid the absolute blackness and the screams, each night brought its own unique terror. The knowledge that the foxhole he had dug with his own hands might well become his grave prompted Wallace to think soberly.

"I knew every night that I might die," said Wallace.

The grandson of a Baptist preacher, Wallace had attended church with his parents and his brother, Richard. "I liked church," said Wallace, "but I didn't like Sunday school. We sat in a circle and read the Bible aloud. I was a poor reader—I still am—and I always got the parts with the big words, and I didn't like stumbling over the words."

But those words returned to him in his Pacific foxhole. "Jesus visited me there in my foxhole," said Wallace.

"It was like I heard the Lord speak to me, saying, 'I am the Way. I stand at the door and knock.'"

Wallace cried when those words came to his mind. "I knew there were two places that I could go if I died: I could go to heaven to be with the Lord and have a pretty good time or to hell and be tormented forever."

He had never accepted Jesus' sacrifice for his sin nor had he asked Jesus to be his Lord. However, in the foxhole, he did just that. "A calm came upon me and I was no longer frightened," said Wallace. "I can't explain it. I never feared any more. I knew my mother and my sweetheart were praying for me, and it was like God wrapped a cloak of protection around me right then."

Although Wallace remained a combatant at Guadalcanal, one of the most ferocious battles of the Pacific War, with death all around him, he emerged the following February without injuries of any kind.

However, the battles in the Pacific theater of World War II were just beginning for the Allies and for Wallace, too. On November 20, 1943, Wallace and forty-five men in his platoon were dropped from Higgins boats in the ocean six hundred yards off the island of Tarawa. This tiny coral atoll was a Japanese-held fortress. Covered by a thick thatch of palm trees, it was guarded by some forty-eight hundred battle-hardened, determined enemy defenders.

The name Tarawa was to stand beside Concord

Bridge, the Alamo, Little Big Horn, and Bellau as one of the great battles fought by the servicemen of our nation. It has been called the shortest, bloodiest battle fought for the smallest speck of land. Said Wallace: "There was no protection for us but the ocean around us. The enemy was crisscrossing the water with machine-gun bullets and there was no escape. I could hear the people around me being shot."

Once he reached the shore, he made his way to safety through obstacles and barricades. The beachhead was covered with the dead and dying. Only fifteen men from his entire unit had escaped the Japanese barrage, but the cloak of protection from the Lord spared Wallace once again. "I truly believe the Lord was with me," said Wallace. He not only survived the beach landing, but also spent the next seventy-six hours in battle, again surviving without a scratch.

As part of the "island-hopping" campaign across the central Pacific, Wallace was again called upon to be part of an amphibious landing on the beach in Saipan. On June 15, 1944, he was among the third wave of marines who landed. Once again the enemy was raking the beach with machine-gun fire.

"I made it across the beach and was hiding behind a log," Wallace remembered. "I could see where the enemy bullets were coming from a bunker, so I threw two grenades at it. I followed the grenades into the bunker and finished the job." Again, while many of his comrades died, Wallace was not injured.

A short time later, Wallace was moved to the island of Tinian on July 24, 1944. While the war in the central Pacific was nearly won, Wallace was still in harm's way as part of a reserve platoon charged with reinforcing the Allied line at battle hot spots.

He recalled a midnight battle in which the Japanese were trying to overrun American artillery units. The enemy was throwing grenades all around them, but in the darkness, the marines couldn't see where to fire. God's protection was particularly sovereign that night, for neither Wallace nor any of his platoon was injured.

As Tinian was falling to the United States forces, Wallace was assigned to the units cleaning out the now desperate Japanese forces from the island's caves. The enemy was still armed and dangerous, and snipers regularly fired at the marines.

"I heard a shot behind me," said Wallace. "I looked around me and saw a corporal grinning at me. He had shot a Japanese concealed in a cave who had a pistol aimed at my back. I thought, *Thank You, Lord! You saved me again!*"

During his four amphibious landings, subsequent battles, and the Battle of Guadalcanal, Wallace's only injuries were a scratch on one finger and a slight shrapnel wound in his back. Wallace believes the Lord provided this unusual protection over him because He wanted Wallace to witness to His saving grace, both on the battlefield and in the lives of men.

Postscript
Wallace remained in the United States Marine Corps for six years and said he tried to witness to all the marines that he could. He joined as a private and was mustered out as a captain and company commander in Peking (Beijing), North China.

While many soldiers had "foxhole conversions," only to abandon their faith during peacetime, Wallace believes he has remained faithful to the Lord because he was reared with Christian principles and because of the prayers of his sweetheart and mother.

Now retired from Keystone Steel and Wire Company after thirty-three years of employment, Wallace is the director of volunteers for a Presbyterian congregation in Peoria, Illinois. He and approximately fourteen retired professional tradesmen spend every Wednesday doing repairs for the poor. Wallace married his sweetheart, Maxine, fifty-four years ago while he was still in the marines. They have a son and four grandchildren.

*A*s the sins of the fathers are passed from generation to generation (Exod. 20:5), it appears that a father's heart toward God may be similarly passed down to his children. Not that God has grandchildren, but faith nurtured, life lessons taught, and godliness modeled will stick with the child into adulthood who was "trained in the way he should go" (Prov. 22:6).

In this story, God healed a young boy of a reoccurring childhood illness. Now an adult and father, he turns to the Great Pediatrician to heal his own seriously afflicted son, once again claiming the same scriptural promise (James 4:13–15) his own mother had claimed many years earlier. The God who is the same yesterday, today, and tomorrow provided the same result.

LIKE FATHER, LIKE SON

Carl Binkley has experienced numerous incidents of miraculous healing in his long life. The first occurred when he was a child of eight.

Carl said his early years were characterized by frequent vomiting spells. Occurring as often as six times a year, they were so severe and debilitating they would keep him out of school for a week at a time.

Said Carl: "I was lying on a cot with such a sickness when our pastor and an evangelist came by for a visit. The evangelist asked Mother if he could pray for me and she said yes. I don't remember anything he said in the prayer, but I was impressed that it was brief, because in those days, preachers made long prayers. After they left, I remember that I got up and played. I never had another of those sick spells."

When Carl was a grown man, he became a pastor. Eventually, he decided to preach a sermon on the work of the Holy Spirit. "I remembered the healing, so I drove up to see Mother and asked about it. She said, 'Yes, you got up immediately and began to play and never had another one of those spells.'

"I used the story of the healing as an illustration in my sermon. Afterwards, five people shyly came up to me and said that they, too, had experienced a miraculous healing but had never told anyone, as they feared people would accuse them of exaggerating."

Many years later when his own young son Timothy lay gravely ill with Stevens-Johnson syndrome, Carl had cause to remember his own healing.

Tim's illness had begun with a simple sore throat. The doctor treated it with an injection of penicillin. Then large open sores began to appear inside the boy's mouth. They spread down his throat, almost totally obstructing his esophagus. Barely able to swallow, he could neither eat nor drink.

Eventually, Tim was admitted to the hospital. The doctors there believed Tim's condition to be a severe allergic reaction to penicillin and didn't offer him much hope of recovery. His condition rapidly deteriorated when he began to bleed through the kidneys. Blood from the kidneys colored his urine. Tim's mouth and throat were ulcerated and swollen. The doctors seemed unable to help. They sent him home with simple instructions: Tim should try to drink a lot of water. However, he could barely swallow his own saliva.

In accordance with the Scripture that instructs the sick to call for the elders of the church to anoint them with oil, lay hands on them, and pray the prayer of faith (James 5:14–15), Carl asked an elder from his church and a neighboring pastor to come to the house. The elder and the pastor touched Tim's head with a small amount of oil. Both laid their hands on Timothy's thin, wasted body, bowed their heads in prayer, and asked God to heal him. When the men left, they were weeping with joy. They believed God would answer their prayer according to His word.

Before their cars were out of sight, Tim made a surprising request. He asked for a bottle of a lemon-flavored soft drink. Since Tim had not been able to swallow anything without a great deal of pain, Carl told his son, "Tim, you can't drink that! It burns the throat of a healthy person."

However, since the boy insisted, Carl drove down to the truck stop and bought a bottle of the soda. Tim drank it with ease and soon was completely recovered.

Postscript
When Tim's illness occurred, doctors told Carl and his wife that if by chance Timothy recovered, he would be

plagued with frequent episodes of bleeding through his kidneys for the rest of his life.

Timothy is now forty-five, married, and has two children. He's never had a reoccurrence of his illness.

*H*ere's a mathematical equation that not everyone learns in school but that Jesus demonstrated for His disciples: 5 loaves + 2 fishes x Jesus = 5,000 fish dinners, R: 12 baskets (John 6:1–13).

In the present day, the math still computes.

Multiplying Stickers

Mid-July 1997

Carol Bjorling was the vacation Bible school teacher for the kindergarten class, with an average of nine squirmy five- and six-year-old students. Although she planned to instruct her students using many lessons during the week, God chose to enlighten her with a miraculous one.

"I was teaching on the theme of the power of prayer and God's provision for us. Our story was about the little boy and the fishes," said Carol. In this famous Bible story, a young child gave his meager lunch—five loaves and two small fishes—to Jesus. Jesus blessed the food and multiplied the lunch to feed five thousand.

Drawing upon her imagination and organizational skills, Carol contrived an object lesson to help her teach the story. She put exactly eighteen stickers in a paper bag. What she planned to do was to give each of her nine students one sticker. The children would then deposit their stickers back in the bag and Carol would "multiply" them and give back to each child two stickers. Carol thought this would illustrate what happened in the Bible story.

When her class convened, Carol discovered that she had two additional students, but she lacked time to add stickers to the bag. "Even though I knew there weren't enough stickers in the bag, I went ahead with the object lesson anyway," said Carol.

She handed out eleven stickers, then told the children how the little boy gave his lunch to Jesus. At that point, she had the students "give" their stickers to her as she collected them in the bag. She told how Jesus prayed over the lunch. Then she handed the bag to a child to redistribute them to her small pupils.

"As the little boy passed out the stickers, I said, 'When we give things away in Jesus' name, God gives us more back.' The kids spontaneously started giving their stickers away to each other."

For a brief moment, Carol lost track of how many stickers were circling the table until her little helper reached the bottom of the bag and asked, "Does everybody have two stickers?"

Said Carol: "Everybody held up their hands and

they all had two stickers! Where did the extra stickers come from? It had to be Jesus! I was going to amaze them—but I was the most amazed!"

Carol Bjorling and her husband, Russell, live in rural Altona, Illinois, where they farm fourteen hundred acres. They have two daughters.

There are two tragedies that can scar a woman's heart for a lifetime: One is discovering that the man she loves is unfaithful. The other is learning that she cannot bear a child. Does God care?

For Isaac, God miraculously arranged circumstances so he could find Rebekah (Gen. 24), the love of his life. When Rebekah couldn't bear children, Isaac asked God to intervene (Gen. 25:20–26)—and He sent twins!

When a young woman in Illinois trusted God to heal her heartbreak, He sent a godly husband. When she couldn't conceive, He sent three babies.

DOUBLE MIRACLES

Perhaps Nancy Anderson found Larry so attractive because he was forbidden fruit. Her father did not approve of him, maybe because he was older and "had a way with women." At any rate, when she was seventeen years old, Nancy fell deeply in love with Larry for reasons she cannot describe. Said Nancy, "He was tall and had a nice build. He drove a navy blue Plymouth that was jacked up in the back. And I loved him."

Nancy was tall, skinny, studious, religious, and rather serious. She had dated numerous boys, but every relationship ended the same way: Her younger sister Pat stole them away; she even shamelessly took Nancy's prom date, leaving her in the lurch on the big night. For one so young, Nancy had already experienced her share of "man trouble."

But Larry steadfastly shunned Pat's flirting advances, leaving Nancy to conclude that here was a man who really loved her and her alone. But while Nancy saw something special in Larry, her father emphatically did not.

"My father is a wonderful Christian man who lives his faith. He was praying that I would meet a good Christian man," said Nancy, "and he thought Larry was no good. He knew Larry had never held a job for more than six months at a time."

While her father's opposition kept Nancy from rushing into marriage, it didn't prevent her from becoming deeply involved. "This was the only time I saw my father really angry. He thought Larry was taking advantage of me. He was going to throw me out of the house, but my mother talked him into sending me to college, where hopefully I would meet someone else."

Away at school, Nancy still saw Larry every weekend. Many of her friends were planning marriage, so Nancy decided that perhaps she should, too. Although Larry duly presented her with a ring, in the back of her mind was the restraining hand of her father's disapproval.

"I knew my father was praying for me," said Nancy. "I just couldn't go through with the marriage knowing that my dad—who likes everybody—did not like Larry and that Larry wasn't a Christian."

Meanwhile, Nancy tried hard to ignore the stray bits of evidence that Larry was dating other women. But after six years of dating, Nancy was irrevocably confronted with the awful truth: Larry was seeing other women—many of them—and he had been for some time. Angry and crushed, she returned his ring.

This began a lonely, uncertain time for Nancy. Her college classes were winding down and she would soon graduate as a medical technician. Nearly all of her friends had wedding plans, and Nancy felt left out, brokenhearted, and rejected.

Until this time, she had maintained a superficial relationship with Christ. "I thought, *I'm a Christian and I'm saved, but I'm young and I want to have fun,*" said Nancy. Now, however, sorrow and heartbreak made her ready for a more serious commitment to Him.

"I was tired of being used. I went to Jesus in tears and prayed, *Bring someone into my life that will love me for being me. Someone I can please without doing or being someone special.* I left it in God's hands. For three months, I didn't date. I just prayed."

March 1975

College was nearly finished for Nancy. She would soon be ready to launch into her new career. Then, on a weekend visit to her hometown, a school chum fixed her up on a double date.

Nancy remembers that she was wary that night. Between the demands of school and her self-imposed moratorium on dating, she had been cooped up, and she was looking forward to some freedom. She did not want any attachments, since she was looking forward to starting to date again.

However, that night, Nancy was introduced to Lynn Sutton. She had no intention of falling in love so soon and certainly not with Lynn. "Lynn wasn't a Christian," said Nancy, "but he was nice, almost too nice. It was like dating my brother. I felt like I had known him forever."

When Nancy went back to college to finish her classes, she and Lynn corresponded, and a friendship blossomed. By the time Nancy began her career, Lynn was obviously deeply in love with her. But to Nancy, there was still one big drawback to a committed relationship: Lynn was not a Christian.

"Actually, I didn't know too many Christian boys," said Nancy. "When I was dating, I brought whomever I was dating to church with me, and I took Lynn with me, too. He said that he always knew there was a God just from looking around at nature, but he didn't know Christ."

As his association continued with Nancy, Lynn learned about Jesus from her father and other members of the church. He could see they had something that he didn't. One evening, Lynn prayed with Nancy to receive Christ. Shortly thereafter, he visited the pastor to request baptism.

"When Lynn returned from seeing the pastor, I was

watching TV in the dark," said Nancy. "He walked in and his face was glowing—like Moses' face did when he came down from Mount Sinai. His face glowed for over an hour. Eventually, it returned to normal, but his commitment to Jesus has remained steadfast."

In May 1976, Nancy and Lynn married, bought a house, and settled into a daily routine. Five years of marriage passed quickly and they looked forward to adding children to their family. After a year of unsuccessfully trying to conceive, Nancy joyfully discovered that a baby was on the way. But anticipation gave way to sorrow when she miscarried at three months.

Said Nancy: "I started going to a gynecologist to find out why we were having so many problems. He put me on fertility drugs and I became pregnant and miscarried a second time. At that point, I hit bottom."

In her job at the hospital lab, she saw an almost daily parade of pregnant teenagers and unwanted pregnancies. "I saw moms who wanted their daughters pregnant so they could raise the amount of their welfare checks. I had a stable household and I couldn't conceive. It made me angry with God. I thought, *How unfair of God!*"

The doctors did studies and concluded that Nancy had a progesterone deficiency that would make it difficult, perhaps impossible, to carry a baby to term. This bleak forecast darkened Nancy's usually sunny personality.

Depressed and angry, she called other believers to pray for her.

At this point Nancy realized that she was praying for the wrong thing. She needed to be seeking God. "I prayed that God would help me deal with my depression," said Nancy. "I began to strengthen my relationship with Him and to trust Him with my life. I learned I needed to love Him rather than just consider Him the God of the Quick Answers."

When Nancy began to earnestly seek the Giver instead of only His gifts, her depression lifted. She became pregnant again, and because of the risk of miscarriage, Nancy took a leave of absence, using the time to read and pray.

"I decided to pray for identical twin girls. I thought, if I was going to have a baby, why not two?" said Nancy. "I was also reading a book about Joshua. What a man of faith!

"Eight weeks before I was due, I went to sleep one night praying for twins. Jesus came to me in a dream and told me that I was not having twins, but a beautiful baby boy. He told me not to be disappointed but to be happy because my boy would be very special—and as it's turned out, he is! I forgot my prayer for twin daughters—but God didn't."

After Joshua was born, Nancy went on with her life. When the hospital hours became too long for both mother and baby, she changed careers and bought a real estate office. "I decided my family was complete. I decided I was not going to get all fussed up again," said Nancy. "If I got pregnant, okay. If not, okay, too."

May 1988
Nancy was delighted to learn that she was again pregnant. She waited anxiously to see if she could hold onto the pregnancy past the treacherous first trimester. But this pregnancy was far different. She experienced no problems except one—she was huge!

"Every morning, I was bigger!" said Nancy.

In August, the hospital did a sonogram. On the screen, Nancy could see two round spots. "What're those?" she asked the technician.

"Those are heads. Two of them," was the reply.

They could not determine the gender of the babies from the sonogram, but Nancy knew in her heart they were girls. In January 1989, Valerie and Natalie Sutton, identical twins, were born.

Postscript
Nancy and Lynn Sutton attend the Galva Baptist Church with their three children. Active in the music ministry of the church, Nancy sings in the choir and is a sought-after local soloist. She has recently added a twist to her vocal programs: Her twin daughters sing with her.

Still the broker-owner of Century 21 Sutton & Associates, Nancy Sutton said that the miracles in her life have taught her three important lessons:

God's time is not our time.

Be careful what you pray for since God does answer prayer.

God has a sense of humor.

There are many visions recorded in the Bible; however, we are told to expect an increase in the frequency of them as time propels us closer to Christ's return (Acts 2:17–18). Sons, daughters, old men, women—all sorts of ordinary people—should expect to see visions and not be surprised when they do.

While some of the Bible's recorded visions pried open the secrets of tomorrow, God also used them to direct the confused and comfort the grieving. Another common function of visions was to inspire God's people to reach out to seekers in a specific way.

This is the story of a woman who via a vision was able to help fight a spiritual battle from afar.

GLORY ON THE LINOLEUM

June 1942
Bunker Hill Church of God Parsonage
Buda, Illinois

It appeared to Catherine "Katy" Binkley that the revival services at Bunker Hill Church of God were not going to revive anybody and her grief over this was profound.

The revival services were so necessary for the church, but they really couldn't have come at a worse time. Just a few weeks before the services, the situation that every pastor dreads had erupted in her husband Carl's pastorate: The leaders were fighting and the church was threatening to divide. Katy and Carl had hoped that the revival services would heal and unify Bunker Hill.

However, after four nights of preaching, the congregation sat stony-faced and unmoved. There was a spiritual coldness in the services, the preaching was flat, the people unresponsive and cold. Without a move from the Spirit of God, Bunker Hill would surely split.

Then, too, there was trouble with the evangelist and his wife. Just married, the young evangelist and his bride were more preoccupied with each other than the revival services. The newlyweds were houseguests at the parsonage, and the new bride was not happy about it. Far from the romantic honeymoon she had anticipated, she spent the day sulking and feeling very ill-used. In the evenings, she reluctantly attended the nightly revival services.

Katy wished she could attend the services, but at age twenty-two, she was the mother of four little boys—all under the age of three. Were this not daunting enough, during this revival week, one of the two-year-old twins had developed a painful ear infection, and the baby cried almost constantly with colic.

Said Katy, "I would get very exhausted, but I tried to keep on. I did, too. But God laid such a burden on my heart for souls that I was pressed down with concern. When I could go no longer, I would drop down by my bed and pray—briefly—as I didn't dare not watch my children."

Then came a brief, shining moment that changed lives and perhaps even the future of a congregation.

On Friday evening of that revival week, Katy noted that the parsonage was unexpectedly quiet. Carl, the evangelist, and his wife were at the revival services. Upstairs, the four cribs were full, and at least temporarily, the little occupants were all asleep.

Although Katy was exhausted from the day's work, she still felt a deep concern for the members of Bunker Hill Church. "I decided that praying was all I could do for them, and the more I thought, the more the concern grew. I went out into the big kitchen and began to pray for the services at church."

What happened next has remained a unique experience in Katy's life. Although she began praying while sitting at the table, her concern grew so heavy that she soon found herself lying prostrate on the linoleum floor, continuing her supplications before the throne of the Almighty.

Suddenly, she "saw" the inside of the Bunker Hill Church of God. The church windows were standing open to receive the night air. In a pew, she noticed a young, nice-looking man with dark hair. She didn't know him, but she knew he needed Jesus.

In her vision, she saw him walk up to the altar and announce that he wanted to make Christ the Lord of his life. Recalling the moment, Katy said, "I was so happy that he came forward. I thought, *Here's a young life for God!*"

Then Katy "saw" some of the church members throwing packages of cigarettes out of the open windows. She understood what their actions meant. They had determined that they would live for Christ and were discarding bad habits. Although the evangelist did not preach, she saw the altar full of praying people who were rededicating their lives to Christ's service and asking forgiveness for their wrongdoing.

Said Katy: "It seemed that I was there at the service. I began to cry and weep and pray for souls. Then God gave me peace about it all and I began to laugh." She felt such a release that she was praising God when she heard a car in the driveway and footsteps on the front porch.

It was Carl, the evangelist, and his wife. They jubilantly began to relate the details of the service. Before they could get too far, Katy stopped them. "I know," she told them. "I was there."

She related in detail what she saw: the young man at the front of the church, people throwing their cigarettes out of the windows, then kneeling to rededicate their lives to Christ. She also knew that the evangelist had not preached.

"How did you know?" they asked repeatedly.

"I was there," she told them.

Katy does not understand everything about her vision, but she knows God showed her "in the spirit" what was happening at the church building several miles away. "I shall always believe that somehow I was there; I can see the service yet in my mind's eye as I was praying.

I still know I was there, but God gave me that experience because I was so concerned for souls, yet I needed to be with my babies.

"I never had an experience like it before or after," Katy said. "Sometimes, I have wished I could have another experience like that one, but I have not ever had the burden for souls that I had at that time."

Postscript

Catherine "Katy" and Carl Binkley said that the young man who gave his life to Jesus in the services described above was not from Bunker Hill Church and they have lost track of him.

The Bunker Hill Church of God, Buda, Illinois, is still a growing congregation. Long ago, it outgrew the building described in the above narrative, and at this writing, it is contemplating erecting yet another facility.

"Many of those people who went there at the time of the revival still attend Bunker Hill," Katy said. "We hear from them sometimes."

Carl and Catherine Binkley, now of Markle, Indiana, are retired from the pastorate but remain active in their local church. Both minister to the area elderly.

When King Ahab and his queen, Jezebel, displayed their arrogance by systematically killing the prophets of God, the prophet Elijah prayed that no moisture would fall on Israel until the king learned his lesson (1 Kings 17:1). It not only didn't rain, but the dew quit falling. When Elijah prayed for the rain to begin (1 Kings 18:41–45), it did.

Locked in a Confederate prison camp, a group of Christian believers asked God to send drinking water into their drought-stricken prison. While they prayed, God answered.

HIGH WATER IN HELL

August 1864
Andersonville, GA

It was as if twenty-six and a half acres of hell were transplanted to Georgia.

On Andersonville's flat, treeless field of red clay, ten thousand Union soldiers milled about, buffeted alternately by freezing and scorching elements. Many were naked and desperately ill. All, including the prison guards, were edging toward starvation. Only disease and vermin were thriving.

In the heat of August, a torrent of prisoners added to the prison population, swelling the number to thirty-two thousand, stretching even farther the thin chord of life to which the soldiers clung. One of those prisoners was eighteen-year-old Private David Smith, Column 4,

First Battalion of the Pennsylvania Volunteers.

At the Battle of Piedmont, Virginia, David had been grievously wounded, shot ear to ear through the head. Bloody, covered with flies, unconscious, and mistaken for dead, he lay on the battlefield for three days and nights. Eventually, he was discovered and taken to Staunton, Virginia, where Confederate soldiers captured him. Then the events in David Smith's young life took a turn for the worst: He was sent to Andersonville Prison.

Although every human comfort was denied the prisoners, terrible thirst was the worst torment. Not that the prison wasn't supplied with water. A thin, sluggish, thoroughly polluted creek, a conduit of disease and death, meandered through the stockade, giving the prisoners an awful choice: Drink and take your chances with a multitude of plagues; abstain and die from thirst.

Wrote David Smith: "Our supply of water was abominably filthy—beyond all description. I could attempt to describe it—but—I cannot without giving you needless offense and pain. During the month of August our suffering for water was very great."

Numerous contemporaries of Smith have verified what happened next. Like nearly all miraculous occurrences, some historians have difficulty attributing the events to the hand of God, although for eyewitness Private Smith, there could be no other explanation.

Wrote David Smith: "Now occurred one of the strangest happenings of my prison life. Famished for food, consumed with the indescribable fever of thirst, a few faithful Christians resolved to test the power of prayer. In their rags and wretchedness, and with tongues blistered by thirst, they prayed the God of heaven to send them water. And lo, while on their knees in the crawling sand, the clouds gathered and the rain gushed down in a refreshing shower. It was a terrific thunderstorm, in the nature of a waterspout."

Astounded prison guards watched this phenomenon from sentry boxes atop the stockade. They saw the whirling cloud and gushing water cleanse away some of the filth of the camp, but they also saw that the security of the prison was breached.

From Smith's writings: "I heard the cannon from the fort firing signal guns, and I crept out of my cave and saw that part of the stockade where the prayer meeting was going on was swept away by the flood, and there was a line of battle formed to prevent the prisoners from rushing out through the opening thus made."

Then came the answer to the thirsty soldiers' prayer in the form of a spring that henceforth provided the camp with a supply of much-needed fresh water. David Smith wrote: "It was at this time Providence Spring first appeared, and it flows to this day, an everlasting testimonial to the power of prayer. It was the end of our suffering for water." If you visit the site of Andersonville Prison, you will see Providence Spring.

David Smith survived both the head wound and Andersonville. He was exchanged November 20, 1864, at Savannah, Georgia. After his release from Andersonville, Smith served with the Union Army until his discharge on June 13, 1865.

Postscript

The year before his internment in Andersonville, Private David Smith played a minor role in an episode forever etched in the American memory.

According to family oral history, on November 19, 1863, Smith was serving as a guard-at-arms to President Abraham Lincoln. The president, besieged by the responsibilities of his office, begged for a half-hour alone in his hotel room to prepare the speech that he was to give later that day.

Once everyone was evicted, Smith stood outside Lincoln's door while the president toiled away inside. A short time later, the door opened and Lincoln asked young Smith to listen to his speech. Holding two sheets of paper, Lincoln read to him the extraordinary words of the Gettysburg Address.

"What do you think?" the president asked.

Smith later recalled that he privately thought the speech was brilliant, but perhaps too short.

After the guns of war stood silent, Smith married a teacher and eventually fathered four sons and one daughter, all of whom graduated from the Conservatory of Music, Philadelphia. Smith became a professor of history, wrote, and lectured on the Civil War.

While the terrible war did not take his life then, the effects of carrying a bullet in his head caused him to have episodes of dizziness. At fifty-two years of age, while trimming a cherry tree, Smith experienced one such occurrence and fell. The results of the fall took his life.

David Smith's account of Andersonville's Providence Spring was written out longhand in manuscript form and is in the family's possession.

*O*ne day in the synagogue, in the midst of an argument over a point of law, Jesus saw a worshipper with a withered hand. The man's concern was not the minutiae of religious legalism, but how to care for himself and his family. He'd come to God for help. The man didn't ask Jesus for a miracle; Jesus just performed one (Mark 3:1–5).

Bonnie's household was divided and unruly. She and her husband were fighting and her children were at war with one another. Then her hands mysteriously became crippled. When she committed her way to God, He miraculously provided a special healing for her and her family.

In God's Hands

As a young housewife in her twenties, Bonnie Kostrewa felt that she had more trouble than she knew how to handle. She and her husband Jim fought about everything—their children, the finances, and her loneliness. No matter how they tried, they just couldn't seem to talk through their problems. Added to that, their sons were waging battles of their own. It seemed to Bonnie that the two boys argued about everything.

Bonnie turned to a professional counselor for help in coping with her marriage and her sons, but the problems continued.

One day, while hoeing weeds in the garden of their country home, Bonnie's hands froze in a clenched position around the handle. "I couldn't open my hands to let go of the hoe," said Bonnie. "I called to my husband and he slid the hoe out from my hands, but they stayed clasped as if I were still holding onto the hoe."

Bonnie was frightened. "I wondered what next could go wrong with my life."

A physician examined Bonnie, but he had no explanation for her mysterious ailment. "I tried to put it out of my mind since by then I could use my hands again," said Bonnie. "I thought maybe it was just an isolated incident."

Later, back in the garden, Bonnie tried to continue hoeing. Again, her hands clenched around the hoe and locked. "The pain was terrible and I couldn't close or open my hands for several hours. I had all kinds of thoughts running through my head and none of them were any good."

Bonnie worried that she had contracted some incurable disease, a bone disorder, or some weird ailment for which no one would ever find a cure. She wondered what would happen to her children.

Jim tried in vain to comfort her. He repeatedly told her that everything would be fine. Bonnie said she didn't believe him because, "I felt the pain, not him." After everyone went to bed for the night, Bonnie lay awake thinking about her life and the heavy burdens on her shoulders. She felt she could not handle another problem.

"I quietly got up and went downstairs to the family room and sat alone in the corner of the couch for a long time, crying, and thinking," Bonnie remembers. "I got down on my knees in front of the couch and poured out my heart to God. 'Lord,' I began, 'I know You suffered to save us from our sins, but what have I done so bad to deserve this? I haven't been the perfect mother and I can't seem to make things right, but I won't be able to fix anything if I am crippled.' "

In the quiet of the night, Bonnie began to realize what was really important to her. Again, she held up her crippled hands to the Lord and began to pray, but this prayer was quite different than the first, for she was holding her hands up to surrender her problems to Him.

"God, I don't care if I am crippled," she prayed. "You can take my hands. Just please make my family happy. Heal their lives that we may live together in peace and we can be a happy family. I would do anything for that, dear Lord."

Bonnie said that while she wept, she held her hands up for what seemed like forever. Then, suddenly, when her soul was the most desperate and she was exhausted from crying, she felt someone gently take hold of her hands. Her eyes still shut, she asked, "Jim?"

No one answered.

"I slowly opened my eyes," said Bonnie. "Peeking through the tears, I could see that no one was there, yet I couldn't close my hands. They felt so warm. It was just as if Someone was holding them."

Realization dawned on Bonnie that God had heard her prayer. She believes this was His way of assuring her that her prayers for her family would be answered. She waited in the presence of God until the feeling of His hands left. Then she noticed something else remarkable: Her hands were free of pain. She could open and close them normally.

"I ran upstairs and told my husband what had happened," said Bonnie. "He replied, 'That's nice, honey.' I knew he wasn't sure if he should believe that my hands were healed or not."

The next day, still bubbling with joy, Bonnie met with the professional counselor. She couldn't wait to tell him what had happened.

"When I told him, he got very angry. He said, 'You don't need that junk in your life! You need to settle down and do what I tell you!' "

Bonnie replied, "God is exactly what I need in my life." She never returned to the counselor.

Bonnie's sons went on fighting, as all kids do, but she seemed to know how to handle it better. Her relationship with her husband steadily improved and her hands never became crippled again.

"Maybe God just needed to get my attention so I would start listening to Him," Bonnie said. "I asked God into my life, and He has been with me ever since."

Postscript
Bonnie's sons are both grown men now, and they have a strong faith in the Lord.

Yvonne (Bonnie) and Jim Kostrewa live in Green Bay, Wisconsin. Bonnie, a poet, said that their faith in the Lord has seen them through twenty-nine years of marriage.

Hannah's grief over her inability to conceive a child sent her to weep before the Lord. Eli the priest assured her that God had heard her prayer. Confidently, Hannah went home, became pregnant, gave birth to Samuel, and eventually had five more children after him (1 Sam. 1, 2:21).

Kim believed God heard her prayer and was going to send her children. Her only question was: "How?"

GOOD AND PERFECT GIFTS

1989

Kim and Rick Snyder began their marriage knowing that their efforts to produce a family might have to be augmented with intervention from fertility doctors. So, a year after they were married, Kim began treatments. Said Kim: "My mother-in-law told me, 'I feel God will bless you with children.'" Kim believed that He would, too.

But despite pricey procedures, conception just didn't happen. As a high school English teacher, the treatment schedule added pressure to Kim's life.

"For three years," said Kim, "we drove fifty miles one way to see the fertility specialist, sometimes every other day. I would leave at six or seven in the morning to get back before school started."

In the course of treatment, Kim and Rick began

working with two obstetrician-gynecologists and two hospitals. Two surgeries and three artificial inseminations later, and facing mounting medical bills with no baby in sight, depression set in.

"I would ask myself, 'What am I doing this for?'" said Kim. "We tried this for a good three years with no answers. The doctors found a few minor problems, but nothing big. They simply didn't know why I couldn't conceive."

Kim said that she was aware that many people in her church were praying for her. "I had been to the altar many times to ask God for children. And I got a stack of notes from people telling me they were praying."

But during the second year of infertility treatments, Kim said she believed God assured her that He had heard those prayers. "It was like He said, 'You will have children and I will bless you with a family of four because that is the desire of your heart.' Some days it was hard to believe it would happen. I am a journaler and when I look back at the pages I wrote, I can tell I had a broken heart waiting for God to bless us with a child."

However, she found a promise in the Bible that she claimed for her own: "Though the fig tree does not bud and there are no grapes on the vines. . .yet I will rejoice in the Lord, I will be joyful in God my Savior" (Hab. 3:17–18, NIV). Her prayer was, "Teach me what You've got to teach me before You answer my prayer for a family."

"It was the closest time to God ever in my spiritual walk," said Kim.

1993

Disheartened with trying to conceive, Kim and Rick looked into adoption. "I got in touch with several agencies, but it was discouraging," said Kim. "They told me the wait would be two to seven years."

1995

Knowing their struggles to adopt, a friend of the family suggested that they consider a private adoption through Harbor House, a maternity home in Celina, Ohio.

After contacting them, Kim compiled a "life book," or a scrapbook containing family photographs. They featured snapshots of their house, parents, celebrations, and Kim and Rick's various interests. This was a tool that Harbor House and its attorney used to help birth mothers choose prospective families for their babies. On April 30, Kim took their life book to Celina, then went home to wait and pray.

At the end of July, Harbor House's attorney contacted them. "This is an unusual case," the attorney said.

He told them that a young woman still in her early months of pregnancy, "Karel," wanted to meet with them about possibly placing her child in their home. She was planning to go to college on a scholarship and wanted to get everything done before she left for the school year. However, he warned them that because it was so early, she could easily change her mind or something else could go wrong.

A meeting was set up in August between Kim and Rick and Karel and the child's biological father.

"We liked them both!" said Kim. And Karel appeared to be pleased with Kim and Rick, too. Several weeks later, she introduced them to her mother, who had doubts about placing the child for adoption until she met Kim and Rick. She, too, felt that God had chosen Kim and Rick to be the parents of her unborn grandchild.

From then on, Kim was intimately involved in Karel's pregnancy. The two women went to the doctor's visits together, and Kim got to hear the baby's heartbeat and see the ultrasounds. When Karel went into false labor a week before she was due, Kim and Rick sat with her until the pains subsided.

February 27, 1995

The decision had been made to induce Karel's labor on this date. While Kim was in the shower preparing to go to the hospital, the phone rang and Rick answered it.

"Karel is going to have the baby today!" Rick shouted to his wife.

"I know, but it's not for a few hours yet," Kim responded.

"No, you don't understand! The hospital called and said that Karel is in labor and her contractions are two minutes apart." Her pains had begun in the night on their own accord.

Kim and Rick drove through the freezing rain to Coldwater, Ohio, where Rick paced the floor while Kim went into the labor room with Karel and remained by her side for the entire delivery.

"I cried because she was in such pain for me," said Kim. "I cried and cried, but Karel was so strong the whole time. In the pictures that were taken, I look like I had the baby and Karel looks like she just stopped in to visit!"

At 6:14 A.M., Karel gave birth to six-pound, fourteen-ounce, eighteen-inch Elizabeth Joy.

"I wanted Karel to hold the baby first when she was born," said Kim. "I didn't have any fear; I just had love. Overpowering love. It was the most miraculous thing I've ever been part of."

Later that morning, after Elizabeth had her bath and was brought into the room for them to hold, Kim told Karel that she could still get out of the contract. "I told her that I would be horribly disappointed, but I wanted her to be sure. I was scared to death, but someone had told me regarding adoption, 'Your motivation has to be love. Don't do anything out of fear.'"

Although the day had been traumatic for Karel, she said, "No, Kim. This is your baby. I carried it for you.

It was never mine."

Said Kim: "I knew it was ordained by God and that we wouldn't have a problem."

Karel left the hospital that evening at 8 P.M. Elizabeth stayed behind to wait for her parents to come for her.

The next day, Kim and Rick were presented with a photo album that was a pictorial chronicle of Elizabeth's birth. Karel had carefully handwritten the photo captions. Today, Kim uses this as a tool to help Elizabeth understand the process by which she came to be Kim and Rick's daughter.

Said Kim: "My verse for Elizabeth is James 1:17 (NIV): 'Every good and perfect gift is from above, coming down from the Father of the heavenly lights. . . .' "

Postscript

When Elizabeth was four months old, another Scripture promise made an impact on Kim's life, Ephesians 3:20 (NIV): "Now to him who is able to do immeasurably more than all we ask or imagine, according to his power that is at work within us." Kim was pregnant without the aid of fertility drugs.

Karel rejoiced at Kim and Rick's blessing and months later stopped to visit them on her way home from college. They were glad to see Karel for several reasons, most pressingly, because Kim was in labor, and they needed someone to watch the baby. Karel stayed with Elizabeth while Kim was rushed to the hospital to deliver Michaela Lynn.

About nine months later, Kim was again surprised to find Olivia was on the way. At this writing, eighteen-month-old Olivia will be joined in a few months by a little brother or sister. Kim will then have the four children she believes God promised her.

Kim and Rick's relationship with Karel and her family continues. Karel is now a college graduate, married, and active in her church. Kim said that Karel's mother is their adopted grandmother.

Kim is at home with her three daughters and sells baskets. Rick is a grain farmer and basketball coach. They live in rural Ohio.

*W*hen we are obedient to what God wants us to do, we never lack for resources.

When God told Abraham to sacrifice his son Isaac—a popular religious ritual of the idol worshippers around him—God sent an angel to put a halt to it and any subsequent human sacrifices, while miraculously providing the ram for the altar (Gen. 22:1–14). In joy and commemoration, Abraham named the spot, "On the mountain of the Lord it will be provided."

Karla Eberle experienced both mountains and valleys. When she gave birth to an out-of-wedlock baby and surrendered him for adoption, God began a chain of miraculous events in her life that showed her He truly provides when we are obedient.

LABOR OF LOVE

1980

As a high school junior and member of the pompon squad, Karla's unplanned, out-of-wedlock pregnancy was more than an inconvenience; it was a potential embarrassment to her family and something that could scar her reputation forever. Her parents shipped her off to a maternity home in upstate New York. She was to surrender the child for adoption after it was born.

"I was living for myself then instead of living for Christ. I didn't like the maternity home at the time, but it was a very good and safe place."

Meanwhile, rumors of her suspected pregnancy were flying in her hometown of Mendon, Ohio. Karla decided to leave the maternity home to try to prove to everyone that she wasn't pregnant. When asked by the father of the baby if she was expecting a baby, she replied, "If I were pregnant, you would be the first to know." Karla never told her close friends at that point. But she did say to her gym teacher, Debbie Fisher, "All these people are saying I'm pregnant!"

"Well, are you?" Debbie asked her. And Karla confided her secret. Outside of her immediate family and the personnel at the maternity home, Debbie was the only other person who knew about Karla's pregnancy.

When Christmas came, Karla's pregnancy was too advanced to hide any longer. Anxious to see her parents but still wanting to keep her secret, she stayed at Debbie's house for the holidays.

Over Christmas vacation, Karla saw something in Debbie that impressed her. Debbie was a single, divorced mother struggling to rear two small children in a tiny, two-bedroom house. But Karla saw Christ in her.

"She let me have her bedroom and she slept on the couch. I thought a lot about this. I wondered, *Why is she doing this?* Everybody loves their own family, but I was just a student and I couldn't give anything back to her. And that stayed in the back of my mind."

After Christmas, when Karla returned to the maternity home, Debbie stayed in touch by letter and telephone. Around her due date, Debbie came up and drove Karla around on bumpy country roads, hoping to encourage the baby to come so she could be there to emotionally support

Karla during the delivery. Although doctors tried to induce labor on two occasions, nothing happened. Karla's baby was now overdue, and Debbie had to return home.

After she left, a Christian girl in the maternity home invited Karla to attend a Bible study with her. Although Karla didn't know it, her Christian friend had prayed that Karla wouldn't deliver her baby and leave until she made a commitment to serve Christ. She wanted Karla to have Christian influence as long as possible, and she knew that once the baby was born, Karla would be leaving.

At the Bible study, Karla decided to live her life for Christ. The next day, she went into labor.

Sunday, April 11, 1981
Karla's son was born in the evening. She kept her baby in the room with her until she went back home. Two weeks later, she returned and signed the papers for her son to be adopted. It was a closed adoption, but Karla felt good about the choice of the child's new family.

"I knew I had done wrong when I got pregnant out of wedlock, but I thought maybe God had allowed all of this to happen so I could give a child to a family who couldn't have one. I grieved for my baby, but it was normal grief. I always felt like it was a good decision."

Karla's friend and teacher Debbie invited her to attend a Bible-believing church with her that helped Karla stay on track through high school.

Autumn 1982

Karla entered the University of Toledo where she volunteered at a crisis pregnancy center. "I thought, *Hey look! God is using my unplanned pregnancy again in my life!* It helped me with the grieving process."

1987

After leaving college, Karla wanted to start a crisis pregnancy center—but she had met and married a Christian man named Doug Eberle and they were soon expecting their first child.

January 1989
Washington, D.C.

Along with members of the Mercer County Right to Life, Karla and Doug traveled to the nation's capital to attend the yearly rally and march that mourns the legalization of abortion.

"At that time, Doug was ambivalent about abortion," said Karla. "But he was overwhelmed by the number of demonstrators and became pro-life on the spot. He was disturbed because we were marching just one day of the year. He was asking, 'If we outlaw abortion, who's going to help these ladies who are experiencing unplanned pregnancies?' "

Shortly after their return from Washington, Karla was awakened in the night. "God said to me, 'Start a maternity home.' This happened for three nights in a row until I couldn't ignore it any longer."

Karla told her husband, "I'm going to tell you this and you're going to think I'm crazy, but I think God wants me to start a maternity home."

Doug listened thoughtfully, then suggested that Karla lay out her project on paper. As she worked on a plan, she started sharing it with people who had some expertise in the area. "I got questions and feedback, but no one said, 'No. Don't do it,'" said Karla.

Karla approached the local chapter of Right to Life and was told that her timing was perfect. They needed someone to run the crisis pregnancy hot line, conduct pregnancy tests, and support expectant mothers in difficult circumstances.

"I wanted to do all that plus," said Karla. She put together an informal steering committee and waited to see what the Lord wanted to do next.

August 1990
Karla's phone rang. On the other end was a local man whom Karla knew to be an on-fire Christian believer. He had a message for her. "I know where God wants your ministry," he told her. Karla was skeptical, but because she knew he was a man of faith, she and Doug met with him.

He took them to downtown Celina, Ohio, where

they walked the grounds of the small, defunct Gibbons Hospital. It had a for sale sign in the yard. Karla remembers promising herself, "I will never raise my kids downtown or in an old hospital building."

But the man told them, "I have walked around here and prayed on this ground, and this is where God wants your ministry." Reluctantly, Karla called the realtor and discovered that the owner had just taken it off the market; however, the owner agreed to loan Karla the keys so she and the board could look at the building.

Karla asked the board to convene in the evening, but prior to their meeting, she walked through the ruined rooms of the old hospital, praying in every room. "I had determined that if the board was unified, we would buy the building. I really didn't think there was much of a chance of that, as the board had never been unified before."

That evening, as she escorted the board through, Karla explained what she envisioned for each room. Then they prayed on the steps before taking a vote. It was unanimous. They wanted to buy the building to make it a maternity home.

Karla laughed as she numbered her liabilities and assets at that moment. Liabilities: no money in the bank—not even a checking account—no name for the organization, no corporation or structure. Assets: a steering committee comprised of a group of people who thought a maternity home was a good idea and a little monthly support from Right to Life.

"We wanted to rent the building and do the renovation at our own expense," said Karla. "I was to present this to the owner."

The owner had his own plans. "I can't rent it to you," he said. "I just leased it to an organization, so if you want it, you'll have to buy it."

Karla said her initial reaction was relief. "This was my out. I thought all these other people were missing what God wanted to do. I wanted a country house with a white picket fence!"

The selling price of the building was $160,000. "The owner said he would hold the mortgage in trust if we could come up with $30,000 now and a balloon payment later," said Karla. "This was Wednesday and we had to have the money by the weekend. That meant Sunday night to me, but the owner meant by 5 P.M. on Friday. I called everybody and said, 'Start praying. Should we do this or look someplace else?' "

At 3 P.M. on Friday, God and Western Union provided Karla and Doug with answers. God gave them the go-ahead on the hospital building and maternity home. Western Union delivered a money order of $30,000 from an anonymous donor. The mortgage note was signed by 5 P.M.

Postscript

On New Year's Eve 1991, while the renovation work continued, Karla and Doug Eberle and their children moved into the old Gibbons Hospital building. Volunteers did all of the renovation work, with the exception of some contract work for which the home has never been billed.

Named "Harbor House," the maternity home has seen 190 babies into the world as of May 7, 1999.

The identity of the mysterious $30,000 donor was not revealed for another five years. Their benefactress was a woman who loved to give but had been prevented from doing so by her husband. He died shortly before she gave the $30,000.

Karla and Doug Eberle have five children of their own and still reside at Harbor House.

The prophet Hosea had a wife who would not be faithful to him. Some of their children were actually fathered by other men. For a time, she became a prostitute and was eventually sold as a slave. As an example of how God wants to tenderly restore those who stray from Him, He miraculously gave Hosea the love to purchase his wife and be reconciled to her.

Mert Newman and Mary Maddy were only living together, but both sensed that their union could not lead to marriage. Seeds of trouble had already been sown in their relationship that would later yield a harvest of heartbreak. When they did finally marry, that bitter harvest would have destroyed most marriages. However, God intervened to bring a miraculous healing to their relationship.

A Healing of the Hurting Hearts

1972–1976
Mary recalls that from the beginning of their relationship, Mert often ogled other women. He would admiringly mention a former girlfriend and pretend to leave Mary for an attractive girl who happened by. He also made disparaging remarks about their sex life. He was joking, but Mary felt insecure and rejected.

Although Mary loved him, when Mert made fun of her she wished she could find another man that would make Mert jealous. Then he'd know how much it hurt. Eventually, she put her plan into action. . . .

October 1985
Now married for eleven years, both Mert and Mary Newman knew that their union was in deep trouble.

The crisis moment came in the autumn, when Mert sat Mary down and asked her if she'd ever cheated on him.

Mary's mind went back to an incident seven years earlier in Colorado. She had met a man and. . .

Mary hedged. So Mert got a Bible and asked her to swear on it.

"Yes," she told Mert, "there was someone, but I didn't really do anything."

Mert suspected she was lying. Mary knew she was.

March 23, 1986
3 P.M.

It had been one more rough day for Mary Newman. So difficult, in fact, that she planned to be dead in less than an hour by her own hand.

Mary's troubled marriage was only one cause of pain. Her beloved brother was paralyzed in a diving mishap in 1980. Then in 1983, her mother died from cancer. Two years following that, Mary's father had been killed in a car accident. His death had occurred one year ago today. And now Mary planned to take her own life.

Her lie to Mert concerning secret sexual encounters stood between them, damaging their intimacy and trust. Mert had been depressed and suspicious ever since their October confrontation, as if the violation had just occurred that day.

A television show she had seen earlier helped bring

her suicide plans into focus. On the program, a couple asphyxiated themselves in a garage. The method was simple, painless, and effective.

Said Mary: "When I saw that, I thought, *That would be the way to go.*"

Mary made plans to drop her two children off at their grandmother's, return home, and shut the garage door on her pain, problems, and life.

"I was frustrated with being a mother, depressed and devastated with marriage," Mary remembers. "But just before I left with the children to take them to their grandmother's, I was sitting on the edge of my bed and I cried out to the Lord and said, 'Why am I here and what is my purpose for living? I don't understand life or death!' "

Mary saw the bedside Bible given to her by a sister who was an outspoken follower of Christ. Flipping it open, her eyes fell on Ecclesiastes 7:16–17 (NIV). She read, "Why destroy yourself? Do not be overwicked, and do not be a fool—why die before your time?"

"Just like that the Lord told me it wasn't my time to die," said Mary.

She read on to the end of the chapter and was struck by one thought: She was put on earth for the purpose of serving the Lord. There was a reason she was alive and she wanted to know more! She put her suicide plans on a temporary hold.

The next day was Palm Sunday. Although church

attendance was not part of their normal routine, Mary and Mert took their children to church. "The whole service, hymns and all, pointed to Christ. It was just what I needed," said Mary.

On Monday, the day that could well have been her funeral, Mary got down on her knees beside her bed and cried out to Christ, asking Him to be the Lord of her life. "I was afraid to tell Mert what I had done because he would make fun of me," said Mary. When he did find out, his only comment was: "Don't get weird like your sister."

Mary's life, however, underwent such a dramatic change that Mert, too, became a follower of Christ on September 16, 1987. They eventually began conducting marriage workshops for other couples with troubled marriages.

While their marriage had improved tremendously, Mary's suspected adultery and lie still stood between them. Mary knew God had forgiven her, but Mert was still troubled by suspicions. "Between us was the lie of adultery," said Mary. "Mert knew in his heart there was adultery."

Over and over again, they would be sitting on the couch watching television while Mert rubbed her feet. When something on adultery would be mentioned, he'd stop. Worse yet, he followed Mary, questioning her activities.

Valentine's Day 1991

Mary recalls that she and a girlfriend were at the dining room table planning a Bible study. When the subject of divorce and adultery was raised, Mert looked directly at Mary and asked, "Did you commit adultery?"

"I couldn't lie," said Mary. "I couldn't pretend anymore. My friend knew the truth, but I didn't think Mert would forgive me because he was always so hard on me." However, Mary quickly admitted the truth. She went on to tell Mert what he never suspected: She had been molested as a child. She had carried that secret throughout their marriage, and he could now see how it had impacted their relationship.

"He felt so bad about the molestation," said Mary. "He kept saying, 'I just needed to know the truth.'" It was a beautiful Valentine's Day.

While healing continued in their relationship, Mary's past would still come up. Mert had suspicions that he didn't know everything, and Mary knew he did not.

Valentine's Day 1992

As Mert and Mary continued to conduct marriage seminars, Mary said she felt urged by the Holy Spirit to tell Mert the whole truth. As she contemplated this, she prayed, *If you want me to tell Mert, let him come home in the next ten minutes.*

"Well," said Mary, "he came home in two!"

Mary said when she told him about the other incident of adultery, Mert began to call her all kinds of names. "It didn't matter what he said or what he called me. I could look in his eyes and not look away. I told him, 'You can call me all those names, and they are true, but I'm forgiven. I'm free. I have nothing else to hide.'"

Mary said Mert battled with this newfound revelation for three days. On the third day, at dawn, after crying all night, he told her, "It's finished. I've forgiven you."

Mary said that her confession to Mert set her free from all of the bondage of the lies and left them free to be able to minister to other people. She said it eventually made Mert aware that his rejection of her was the catalyst for her adultery. He needed to ask her for forgiveness as well.

He said, "I realize I wasn't a good husband to you." Mert also realized that he was wrong for never forgiving Mary. He would never mention her adultery again.

"By not telling him the truth," Mary said, "I was hurting the marriage. By telling him, we had surgery and God healed us."

Mert and Mary Newman jointly own and operate an excavating business, Newman Leasing, Inc., Kewanee, Illinois, and continue to teach in marriage workshops. They have two children.

In Jesus' day, the orthopedic surgeon's office was a pool outside the Sheep's Gate called Bethesda. Surrounded by five columns, disabled people lay around it hoping that an angel would stir the pool's waters. If that happened, the first person in was supposed to be healed. It didn't happen often, but it was all they had.

Jesus spoke to a crippled man who had been waiting beside the pool for thirty-eight years in hopes of a healing. "Do you want to be healed?" He asked him. The man began to mutter excuses, but Jesus told him to get up and be healed. When the man took that first step of faith and rose to his feet, he was healed (John 5:1–9).

Michelle Robison's injury would not wait thirty-eight years for a healing. If God didn't do something soon, she would die. Then she reached out and took hold of God's promise.

IN THE NECK OF TIME

November 8, 1989, 11 P.M.
Northwestern Ohio

Michelle Robison's need for a miracle came about late one evening when she and her brother were riding in Michelle's car. The night was very dark and rainy as Michelle drove home from an antique car club meeting. Snug inside, the windshield wipers slapped back and forth against the wet drizzle. They were so engrossed in conversation that Michelle drove past Domersville Road, the turnoff to her brother's home.

"Oh! You missed my turn!" her brother said.

Michelle thought that since her brother often spent the night with her and her husband, he could do so tonight. As they entered Carpenter Road, she turned to her brother to tell him that she would take him home tomorrow—and then everything went black.

Michelle's life was changed forever when a woman driving home from work ran the stoplight and collided with Michelle's car. The side impact shattered the driver's side window, drove in the door about a foot, and caused Michelle's seat belt to disengage. Her car spun around and impacted with a road sign, but the centrifugal force forced Michelle out the driver's side window, tearing off the top of her scalp. Michelle bounced on the pavement several times before she came to rest seventy-five feet from the car. Every window in the car was broken except one.

Although her brother was not wearing a seat belt at the time of impact, he was uninjured. When he found Michelle's still form lying bleeding on the edge of the road, he was amazed to discover she was still alive.

Several hours later. . .
Although she felt nothing at the time of the accident, Michelle was in a good deal of pain when she regained consciousness in the emergency room. "I woke up to find the emergency room personnel sewing me together," said Michelle. "I was shocked to find myself bloody and naked, with people holding me down."

Eventually, Michelle was admitted to the small-town hospital where she was brought following the accident. Head and chest x-rays were ordered, but as her care was shuffled between an emergency room doctor and the hospital physician, Michelle's most serious injuries were left undiagnosed.

Thinking that her wounds were only lacerations, the doctor prepared to release her the following day. With blood dripping down her face where her scalp had been reattached, Michelle told her doctor she had a terrible headache.

"The doctor yanked the bandage off my head and looked at it and said, 'You're okay!' and released me," said Michelle. She walked out of the hospital with an undiagnosed broken thumb, a broken neck, and fractured skull.

November 12, 1989
Four days later, Michelle went back to the doctor for a follow-up visit. Said Michelle: "My neck and head were hurting very badly and my vision was going. I had a strange electric shocking feeling when I lifted my arms."

"You're fine," the doctor assured her, but Michelle wasn't so sure. Because of her ever-increasing disability, she switched doctors—and her new physician immediately ordered a CT scan. It revealed not only the broken thumb and skull fracture, but also a potentially deadly break in her spine.

The day before Thanksgiving, Michelle received the bad news: She had a quarter-inch fracture in her second cervical vertebrae, where the nerve endings that control pulmonary function are housed. A false move and Michelle's heart could stop. Because of her skull fracture, she couldn't be fitted with a halo brace, but a less effective neck brace was applied.

There was little point in readmitting her to the hospital, the doctor told her. The bones in her neck simply needed to heal. Hopefully, time and natural healing could accomplish this; an extremely risky surgery would be the only other alternative. Because of the location of the break, the surgery would require entry through the front of the neck, working around all of her arteries and veins to fuse her spine.

To make matters worse, Michelle's skeletal system was already overtaxed as she was in remission from bone cancer. "Go home, lay in your bed, and don't do anything," the doctor instructed her. His words concerning her prognosis were less encouraging: "You'll either live or die."

For the next four months, Michelle was locked into a neck brace, afraid to move, afraid to swallow, afraid to sneeze. "I went back and forth between asking, *Why did this happen to me?* and wondering what I did to deserve this," said Michelle. "I wasn't blaming God, I just wondered. Eventually, I thought, *I can sit around and feel sorry for myself or I can go back to my college classes.*"

Michelle decided that she could sit quietly and listen

to her professors and do her homework, hopefully without further injury to herself. "My appearance was shocking," said Michelle. "I came into class with a neck brace and I looked like Frankenstein's mother. I had a bald spot on my head and between two and three hundred stitches."

While Michelle was struggling to live, her prognosis was diminishing. Even though her white blood cell count soared and her bone cancer stayed in remission, the CT scans revealed that she wasn't healing.

"The bone in your spine is dying," the doctor told her, then reviewed her options. "You can have surgery to fuse the vertebrae, but you'll have to sign a waiver that you understand that your chances of surviving the surgery are nil. Or you can wear the neck brace until the bone rots and you die." Either way, Michelle knew that death was stalking her.

At this point Michelle's mother went to talk to the elders of the church. They agreed to lay hands on Michelle and anoint her with oil (James 5:14–15). "I can't even remember what they prayed or what I prayed. I basically asked God to heal me. I told Him that I wasn't greedy. I didn't care if I hurt; I just wanted to live. When they were done praying, I felt at peace," said Michelle. "After that, when I would start to worry, I'd tell God I was sorry."

About ten days after the anointing, Michelle had

another CT scan and then returned to the doctor. Up on the light box were two scans: The first was a previous x-ray that clearly showed the break; the other x-ray showed the bones joined.

"I thought this would be the one doctor who would understand what had happened," said Michelle, "because I knew he went to church and was religious, but he thought we'd switched x-rays with someone else."

"This is a joke, isn't it?" he accused.

Michelle had a difficult time convincing him that the new x-ray truly was hers. She was healed.

"The elders laid hands on me and prayed for me," Michelle told him.

"Well, there's nothing wrong with you. You're fine," he told her.

"Aren't you going to take the neck brace off?" Michelle asked.

"No, you can take it off yourself," he said and left the room.

Once in the car, Michelle's husband questioned her about her doctor's visit.

"When we get home," she answered joyfully, "you can take the brace off me!"

He couldn't wait that long, so he took the brace off in the car. The last time Michelle had her brace off, she had to literally hold her head in her hands, but this time, while her neck was weak, she could hold her head up. "It was hard to hold it up because it felt so heavy on my neck. Instead of a head, I felt like I had a bowling ball there," said Michelle.

Postscript

Michelle believes that not everyone can accept healing. "I really don't know why God chose to heal me, but I think it was because I asked. Also, I like to talk a lot and He knows I'll tell people. I think it was to help somebody somewhere," said Michelle.

Michelle started to make dolls after her car accident. "I gave the first one to the woman who hit me. I think it is easier to be the victim than to be the person who caused the accident. The other woman couldn't shake the image of my accident. I had no ill feeling toward her. The money that the lawyer felt I should have gotten from the lady I have made from making and selling dolls. That is something else God brought out of it," said Michelle.

Michelle's husband, John Alan, is a factory worker and Michelle is a full-time doll maker. They live near Napoleon, Ohio.

When God's people needed food, He rained manna down from heaven with the dew and sent flocks of quail. They all had as much as they needed (Exod. 16:11–18).

When Norma Bennett discovered that her neighbor and family were going hungry, she didn't know how to provide for their many needs. But she knew the God who had once covered the ground with groceries for His people could show her what to do. However, she had no idea that she would be God's conduit for bringing two miracles into her neighbor's life.

NEIGHBORING GOOD SAMARITAN

When Norma Bennett befriended "Beverly," a nearby resident who lived in one of the houses behind her, they discovered they had a good deal in common. Not only did they live in the same neighborhood of a small Indiana town and know many of the same people, they both had teenage children. They began to share garage sales and coffee. "We were back and forth at each other's houses all the time," said Norma.

But in addition to enjoying Beverly's companionship, Norma was praying that Beverly would make Jesus Lord of her life. Although Beverly had been reared in the church, she was now far away from God while she tried to cope with a temperamental husband and a young adult son who was mentally and physically handicapped.

Circa December 1, 1981

On a cold, blustery day in late autumn when Norma stopped in to see Beverly, Norma got her first clue that something was terribly amiss in her friend's household.

"I knew her husband was laid off and that she was scrimping, but I could tell the heat was off when I walked in the house. Their house was drafty even when they had heat, but now cold air was lifting the carpet!" said Norma.

A forklift driver for many years, Beverly's husband had been part of a company-wide layoff that had stretched too long for their short finances. "He didn't make good money anyway," said Norma, "and they didn't have any savings. They were so far in debt that the unemployment check didn't cover their needs, and eventually it ran out."

"Don't you have heat?" Norma asked Beverly.

"No," her friend replied, "and no money to get it." Beverly was holding a slice of bread in her hand. "We're eating out of a garbage can." She explained that someone was bringing them the stale bread and wilted fruit that the local grocery was throwing out.

Stunned and concerned, Norma went home and prayed about her neighbor's dire financial condition. "I asked God what to do about this because I couldn't supply all of their needs," said Norma.

After she finished praying, Norma went through her own freezer and cupboard, putting together three or four bags of meat, cereal, and other groceries.

When she took them back to her neighbor's house, she found the family huddled in blankets, sitting around the open door of their gas oven.

"Here's some food for you. I know it won't last," Norma said.

Tears of joy began to flow down Beverly's cheeks. "She was tickled to death that they would have meat for supper," said Norma.

With some of the family's immediate needs met, Norma began to think about what else she could do. Said Norma: "I just started calling all my neighbors and told them what was going on. Then I got together with two neighbors and discussed what they wanted to do. We all felt the family really needed help."

Eventually, Norma began to contact other individuals and organizations besides her neighbors, and miracle after miracle began to happen. "It was just wonderful," said Norma. "Some brought items and money directly to me, and if they knew Beverly, they took things directly to her. Sometimes, she'd call me and say, 'What's going on?' And I'd say, 'Well, what?' And she'd say, 'Somebody left this or that on our porch!'"

Help came as gifts, money, groceries, and shopping trips. Sometimes, Norma knew who the benefactor was; many times, she did not. For example, Beverly's heating oil was replenished. To this day, Norma still does not know who filled the tank.

As the days drew close to Christmas, Beverly and her husband still didn't have any gifts for their daughter, but suddenly gifts for her appeared. Beverly and Norma stood looking at the pile of gifts with tears on their cheeks.

"Just look at all this stuff," Beverly said wonderingly. She was completely overwhelmed.

Said Norma: "I don't think she'd ever been around anybody who gave like this. I was around my mother and grandmother and I saw how to help other people. Now Beverly really learned a lesson."

Help poured in for a good month, long enough for Beverly and her family to get back on their feet. Another "gift" was given to the family when the husband was called back to work in January.

A second miracle happened about the same time: Beverly became a Christian believer. "I could really see the difference in her," said Norma.

Postscript

Norma Bennett said that Beverly has since moved to a neighboring town, so they now have less contact. However, the last time she saw Beverly, she remains strong in her faith in Jesus, in spite of numerous health problems.

Norma and her husband live in Markle, Indiana.

$\mathcal{G}$od is amazing when it comes to keeping track of details. He knows the birds that fall to the ground and the number of hairs that are on your head (Matt. 10:29–30)—a detail that you don't even care about!

When a high official in the Ethiopian court needed help understanding the Scriptures, God sent a man named Philip to a specific spot where they would be certain to meet. The Ethiopian came along in his chariot and Philip noted that the man had a scroll of the writings of Isaiah—a perfect tool for explaining Christ's sacrifice. The man invited Philip to ride along and explain it to him. The Ethiopian came to faith in Christ and asked, "Why shouldn't I be baptized?" just as they encountered a pool of water. The man was baptized, and then God provided miraculous return transportation for Philip (Acts 8:26–39).

When another group of Africans needed help worshipping God, all of the details were worked out by the Divine Planner—including the transportation.

Organ Transplant

Summer 1966
Sierra Leone, Africa

The African mission church had saved two hundred dollars. In one of the poorest countries of the world, this was a princely sum and represented great personal sacrifice for the members of the congregation. They prayed that God would lead someone halfway around the world to an organ that they could use to sing praises to the God of the Bible. But would two hundred dollars be enough to buy an organ in the United States and ship it all the way back to Africa? Another important detail: Since the church lacked electricity, the instrument needed to be one of the old pump organs, the type highly prized by antique dealers and collectors.

Summer 1966
Bluffton, Indiana
4:20 P.M.

Insurance salesman Paul Sell stopped at a house about a half mile from his home. This was his last business call for the day.

He finished with his client and was exiting the house when his eyes fell upon an antique pump organ sitting in the corner. Jokingly he asked, "Does your son play that?"

"No," the woman replied, "and if you know anyone who wants it, I'll sell it for fifty dollars just to get it out of my living room!"

That was a bargain price for a pump organ, but Paul didn't know anyone who wanted it. Or so he thought.

Same Day
About 4:30 P.M.

When Paul showed up a little early for supper, his wife handed him a letter. His name was on the envelope, but he discovered that the message inside was actually meant for Claire, a blind friend who tuned pianos for a living. The letter requested that Claire locate a pump organ for a Christian mission in Sierra Leone, Africa. Enclosed was a check for two hundred dollars. This sum was to cover both the cost of the organ and the shipping all the way to Africa.

Paul thoughtfully regarded the letter. It had been

written by an elderly, retired missionary who spent six hours a day writing to missionaries all over the world and another six hours praying for them. What a challenge accompanied the prayers from this old missionary! Little did Paul realize what would happen next.

Remembering his neighbor's pump organ, Paul picked up the phone. "I'll take that pump organ off your hands," he told his customer.

Same Day
4:40 P.M.
Paul made his next phone call to Claire and told him about the letter and the newly procured pump organ. Claire had an idea how to ship the organ. He knew that the local piano factory shipped pianos in crates. While the pianos were sized and weighted differently than the fragile, old pump organ, Paul and Claire thought the crates might be adjusted to fit it—if only they could get a couple crates!

Claire would call the piano company and see if he could secure some crates. Paul then telephoned Bob, a friend who owned a trailer. "Could you give me a hand sending an organ to Africa?" Paul wanted to know.

Same Day
5 P.M.
Paul and Bob wrested the pump organ from the client's living room onto the back of the trailer, then headed to

the piano factory. As Providence would have it, the piano factory was working second shift that night. The factory had agreed to donate two crates for the organ. All Paul and Bob had to do was come get them.

Same Day
6 P.M.
Paul and Bob picked up the crates and headed back to Paul's garage.

Same Day
6:30 P.M.
Now came the tricky part: How could they pack the pump organ to withstand the rigors of traveling from Indiana to Africa?

The men studied the shape of the crates versus the shape of the organ. With a hammer and a little ingenuity, they made one crate out of two. But the resulting container still did not meet their standards for sturdiness.

Same Day
7:15 P.M.
A phone call to another friend provided them with extra fortification for the crate. He met them at the shipping doors of his manufacturing plant and secured the box with metal bands. Now the crate was sturdy enough to withstand the trip.

Same Day
7:45 P.M.
Bob's son-in-law Dick backed his eighteen-wheeler up to the loading dock of Franklin Electric, Bluffton, Indiana. The freight line for which Dick drove was sending him to Indianapolis that night, and he had room for the organ with his regular load. From Indianapolis, the organ would be routed to a New York port for its sea voyage. All that was left for Paul and Bob to do was to load it on the truck and pay the shipping.

Once the organ was inside the trailer, Dick figured the charges. "It comes to $150 even," he informed them.

Same Day
8 P.M.
Back at home, Paul recounted to his wife the events of the day. "We marveled how everything had turned out. Less than four hours had elapsed since I had received the letter! The evening climaxed with a telephone call to the retired missionary who had sent the letter."

Two Weeks Later
Sierra Leone, Africa
The organ was picked up and delivered to the village, sparking a great rejoicing when the church discovered that they had sent exactly the right amount. Their prayers had been answered!

Paul Sell has been selling insurance for forty-seven years and plans to continue for a couple more. He and his wife, Betty, have two sons and six grandchildren.

It is sometimes hard for people to believe God will heal them, not because they think God is unable, but because they are not sure He is willing to bother with them. A man with leprosy had that problem. He approached Jesus, knelt with his face to the ground, and said, "If You want to, You could heal me."

Jesus said, "I want to," and immediately the man was healed (Luke 5:12–13).

Some people wish to ask God for healing, but they are not quite sure that God is willing to be bothered with their trifling problems. However, God says the same to them as He said to the man with leprosy: "I want to."

BECAUSE HE IS GOOD

Late Summer 1979
Zanesville, Indiana

Not many miracles begin with a sneeze; however, Rose Mary Lampton's did.

The summer was drawing to an end, and Rose's children had returned to school. She was enjoying a quiet moment at the breakfast table with her husband when late-summer allergies made her sneeze. Recoiling, she discovered that she had injured her back and couldn't straighten up. In a lot of pain but amused at the absurd way in which she had hurt herself, she asked her husband Joe to help her to the living room sofa. Rose had experienced backaches since she was a high-school girl, so she thought if she could rest for a time, her back would right itself.

Rose was scheduled to play piano later that morning at the church, a scant three blocks away. She tried to walk the distance, but the pain became so excruciating that a neighbor had to help her home. Eventually, the pain was so bad that she had to be hospitalized.

Rose could not understand why this backache was so painful and persistent. But the orthopedic surgeon at the small-town hospital pinpointed her problem. "I did the surgery on one of your brothers when he had back problems," he told her. "His slipped disk looks just like yours. You're heading for surgery, just like him."

After a week in the hospital, Rose was released to complete bed rest. Although she attempted to stay off her feet and read books, as a mother who was trying to hold a job at the local post office while caring for her family, Rose could not afford to wile away each day in bed.

"I tried to decide I was well, but I had so much pain by the end of the day, it would be just awful," said Rose. "The pain ran down my right leg and would make my toe numb. Joe was working in the evenings and he would get off at nine, but I'd be so exhausted that I'd be asleep by the time he got home. I would think I was sleeping soundly, but I was tossing and turning and moaning out loud. I was making so much noise, he couldn't get any sleep."

One evening a short while later, her father stopped in to see her. Rose was standing at the sink washing the dishes, and she said to him, "Dad, I know you've prayed for my back before, but would you pray for me one more time?"

Rose's father laid his large, callused hand on her and prayed a prayer she has never forgotten. "God, we ask You to heal her not because we're good, but because You're good."

Said Rose: "I thought I could believe now that God could heal me. My silent prayer was a prayer of faith based on the fact that God was good, not that I was."

When Rose walked her father to the door, she noticed that there wasn't any pain down her leg. "I thought at the time, *Maybe it'll come back*," said Rose. "But I put the kids to bed and went to bed myself and slept soundly."

The next morning, she still felt fine. "I wondered, *Is this really happening?* but I didn't want to say anything until I was sure," Rose said.

After two nights without listening to his wife moan in her sleep, Joe called Rose from work. "What happened to your back? You haven't been tossing and turning at night," he asked.

"I think God healed me," Rose told him.

"I knew something happened because you've been sleeping like a log," he responded.

Rose did not have to have surgery nor have her back problems returned. She still has allergies.

Postscript

Rose Mary Lampton's four older brothers have had to have surgery to repair slipped disks, the same back condition from which she believes she was healed.

Rose still works for the U.S. Post Office, Markle and Fort Wayne, Indiana, offices. Her husband Joe manages a Dollar General store and pastors a United Methodist Church. The Lamptons have three children and three grandchildren and live in Zanesville, Indiana.

What do angels look like? Popular artist renderings depict them as chubby little babies or beautiful women. Certainly not fearsome. However, when they are seen undisguised in the Scriptures, the first words out of their mouths are often, "Fear not!"—hardly something a cherubic child or a pretty girl would need to say!

Occasionally in the Scriptures, angels appear as men who have a message of comfort to deliver. Abraham entertained three men who were traveling toward Sodom. Although their appearance was that of normal men, two of them were angels. They reiterated what Abraham already knew: A child of promise would be born in his and Sarah's tent (Gen. 18:1–10).

Does God still send out angels to deliver messages of assurance? Mary Ann Budde believes He does.

ROUTE TO PEACE

Spring 1977

One sunny noon Mary Ann Budde saw an angel. She wasn't looking for one that day. Instead, she was searching for an answer to the problem that had her mind in turmoil.

For the first time in her life, Mary Ann was studying the Bible in preparation for a children's Bible class she was teaching for her church. The passages she read clearly indicated to her that the doctrines of her church were wrong. This presented her with a problem: Should she, her husband, and eight children leave their church?

Said Mary Ann: "I was thinking, *Do I leave? Do I stay? Would the kids go with us?* I kept wondering if that would be the right thing. I knew my mother's heart would be broken if we went to another church. She was an older woman, and I was afraid it would kill her. I knew I would be an outcast in my family."

As Mary Ann drove home on Route 127 accompanied by these thoughts, she did something very unusual for her: She picked up a hitchhiker north of Celina, Ohio. "I just felt like I should pick him up. He looked harmless enough. Just a guy, about six feet tall, normal-looking, with no beard or anything distinguishing. He was wearing blue jeans and a red plaid flannel jacket. I can't remember his face."

Mary Ann's new black Bible—one that she describes as being a "big, fat one"—lay on the dashboard in front of her, and the hitchhiker commented on it. They began talking about the Lord, and Mary Ann said that an unbelievable calm came over her. She recalls that the man talked to her about the words of Jesus as recorded in John 14:27 (NIV): "Peace I leave with you; my peace I give you. I do not give to you as the world gives. Do not let your hearts be troubled and do not be afraid." Mary Ann said that the words went straight to all the turmoil in her life and began a healing and helping process.

But when Route 274, Mary Ann's usual route home, came up, she drove on by. "We just kept talking about the Lord," said Mary Ann. "I just couldn't let him out." Then came Route 119 East, the next possible turnoff to her home, but Mary Ann purposely drove past it, too, deeply engrossed in her conversation about the Lord, enjoying the peace of God.

When they finally reached the little town of North Star, a stoplight made them pause. Mary Ann pulled over. This was the last possible direct route home. She told the man that she had to drop him off.

He got out of the car and said, "Bless you."

Mary Ann said, "My heart was blessed!"

As she turned east and headed her car home, she thought she needed to go back. "I turned around to go back, to wave or something, but I'm not really sure what I was going to do," said Mary Ann. In a matter of moments, Mary Ann was once more in North Star. She scanned the road, but the stranger was gone.

"He would barely have had time to walk across the road, and I would have seen another car if one had stopped to pick him up. I wondered, *Where did he go?* He could not have gone anywhere. He was nowhere in sight and there were no cars."

Mary Ann was filled with peace. "I remembered the verse he had given me and I wanted to get home and read it."

She really didn't think too much of the incident at all until she heard a sermon about angels and how when some people thought they were entertaining strangers, they had actually been visiting with angels. Mary Ann told the Lord, "I would like to see an angel. Why don't I see angels?"

God's voice seemed to whisper, "Don't you remember?"

Postscript
Mary Ann Budde, her husband, Bob, and their eight children did change churches. It didn't kill her mother, who came to live with Mary Ann and didn't die for another twenty years.

The Buddes live in Maria Stein, Ohio, where Mary Ann designs and sells gifts.

We are sometimes tempted to complain when the unexpected happens in our lives. Yet, one of the amazing ways God displays His divine power is to work out the details of our lives better than we can ask or think. This is why Christian believers are instructed to rejoice in everything—because God is in control of situations that seem out of control.

A Miraculous Fact of Life

Millions of Americans watched as Lisa Welchel blossomed into a beautiful young woman on NBC's "Facts of Life." Now pregnant with her second child, she was ready to face some of those facts herself.

"Tucker, my son who was twenty months old at the time, was born cesarean, but I wanted to deliver this child in the normal fashion," said Lisa.

"Once cesarean, always cesarean" had been the rule of thumb for many, many years, but obstetricians, rethinking the procedure, were increasingly telling mothers that the former incision would be strong enough to withstand the rigors of childbirth.

Said Lisa: "The doctor said that there was a .05 percent chance of the scar opening during labor. 'It's not going to happen,' they told me, 'so don't even worry about it.'"

Lisa and her husband, Steve Cauble, planned accordingly. They were looking forward to experiencing natural childbirth right up to the epidural, when they would witness a normal delivery.

September 26, 1991
Early Afternoon
Cedars Sinai Hospital
Los Angeles, California

The moment of truth had arrived. Lisa's pregnancy had been uneventful and there was no reason to suspect that the delivery would be any different.

"All went well until I was just about to push," said Lisa. "Then they determined that the baby was in fetal distress, because the baby's heart rate was vacillating between fast and slow." Unwilling to further stress the baby by a trip through the birth canal, the doctor ordered an immediate cesarean delivery.

"I was very, very disappointed as we had gone through the hard part," said Lisa. "As they were wheeling me into the delivery room, I felt God's Spirit remind me that we were to rejoice in all things. So I prayed, *Thank you, Lord, for this cesarean.*"

Moments later, Haven Cauble, a baby girl weighing in at six pounds and nine ounces, was born. "She was alive and all seemed to be going well," said Lisa.

Steve followed his newborn daughter from the surgical

suite to the nursery. Behind a plate glass window, he watched as nurses began to give Haven her first bath. Suddenly, the scene changed. Nurses began frantically tearing open packages of medical equipment, calling to one another, and paging doctors. Before he could tell what was happening to his child, someone pulled down the window shade in front of him.

Same Day, Late Afternoon. . .

Lisa did not know there was anything amiss with her baby until she was taken back to her room in the maternity ward. Until then, she only knew that she was truly grateful she had had a cesarean, because her labor pains had torn open her previous incision. Had she delivered normally, she could well have hemorrhaged, killing either herself or the baby or both.

Then Steve told her what he had seen through the nursery window. All they knew was that Haven was having trouble breathing and they needed to keep her there. They didn't have any idea how severe her condition really was.

The miracle of Haven's cesarean birth began to be revealed to Lisa and Steve in bits and pieces. Not only were they thankful that Lisa's reopened incision had not hemorrhaged—as it almost surely would have during delivery—but the doctors also told them that Haven's umbilical cord was wrapped around her ankle, something that could have slowed down a normal delivery or even prevented it.

Four days later, Lisa was released from the hospital. She checked into a hotel near the hospital where she could be on hand to nurse and care for the critically ill Haven. Haven was still a very sick little baby.

Not until two weeks later did Lisa and Steve fully understand the miracle demonstrated by Haven's cesarean delivery.

Said Lisa: "Haven had Group B streptococcus, which is often a fatal infection. Some mothers carry it in their birth canal, and they give it to the baby in the birth canal. In Haven's case, the infection went up the birth canal and infected her in utero, but we don't know how, as my water had not been broken for an extended time. We're 99 percent sure she would not have lived if she had traveled through the birth canal. As it was, the infection had gone into the spinal column but not into the brain."

Lisa concluded: "It is a lesson to rejoice in all things."

Lisa Welchel Cauble and her husband, Steve Cauble, have a son and two daughters. At the present, Lisa is a stay-at-home mom, having put her

acting career on hold. Rearing her children in God's Word has inspired Lisa to write a children's book, Beyond Bible Stories, *which is a compilation of some of the great stories in the Bible that are sometimes omitted from children's collections.*

*A*fter the Israelites left Egypt, they traveled through an utter wilderness ominously named the Desert of Sin. Water was a scarce commodity there and a great deal of it was required for so many people and their livestock. Thirsty and cranky, they complained to Moses for not providing sufficient water. Moses did what the people should have done and asked God for help. God told Moses to strike a specific rock. When he did, water gushed out (Exod. 17:1–6).

Sandee Crockett found herself lost and drying up in a desert of ill health. Within this desert, God showed her a Rock that contained refreshing, life-giving Living Water.

WITNESS IN CLAY

Late 1950s

While many little girls love dolls, during Sandee Crockett's formative years, they were her best friends. "My father was a pilot in the air force and we moved every two years. Everywhere we lived, my mother would give me the bottom of a closet where I could play with my dolls," Sandee remembers.

Sandee describes how the little homes she created for her dolls, with cinderblocks as walls and boards for floors, assuaged her loneliness and displacement. There Sandee and her dolls could live in a familiar world of old friends with their own families, mothers and children, all engaged in make-believe activities and dramas.

Sandee's grandmother contributed to her creative play. An accomplished seamstress, she would sew the clothing that Sandee designed for her dolls, letting Sandee choose among her scraps of fabric for just the right piece of material.

Because of their frequent moves, their church attendance was a little sporadic. "Mom was a Christian believer, and she would take me to church. Dad would have pancakes ready when we came home," Sandee said.

During the family's stint in Taiwan, Sandee became involved with a group of missionaries. But when she heard one of the missionaries say that people in the deepest depths of Africa would go to hell because they had never heard the gospel, she seized upon it as an excuse to turn away from God and the church. Said Sandee: "I remember thinking, *That can't be right!*"

1972
Mission Viejo, California
Now a mother of two sons and the wife of a naval officer, Sandee found herself living in a cozy, friendly neighborhood overrun with children the same ages as her sons. She had previously begun a tradition of making a Christmas tree ornament for each of the neighbor kids when she discovered a recipe for bread dough clay. The handmade ornaments she crafted were greeted with "oohs" and "aahs" of delight.

"You should make these to sell at the craft show," she was urged by her amazed neighbors. Sandee took their advice and sold everything she made. This was the beginning of a part-time, home-based job for Sandee. She did two or three craft shows per month during the holiday season, and time and time again she saw her little bread dough ornaments sell out.

1978
Marietta, Georgia
Now in her thirties, Sandee decided to make some changes in her life because she noticed she was gaining weight. While she never exercised much, she had tried to maintain a trim shape. Now she decided that jogging would help her lose a few extra pounds, so she began to run, eventually competing in 10K road races.

About the same time, Sandee began attending aerobics classes. When the gym needed a new instructor, Sandee applied for the job. "It was perfect for me. I had years and years of dance instruction, and I loved to dance but my husband didn't. Now I could move to music and get paid for it!"

Shortly after that, in 1980, she and her husband attended a marriage encounter seminar with their neighbors. "It was here that I made my first real commitment to the Lord," said Sandee. "However, I was just peeking at Him, not surrendered to Him. I was not asking what I could do for God, but what He could do for me."

For the next fifteen years, Sandee's life went along as

she planned. She reared her family, taught aerobics, did a few craft shows with her bread dough ornaments, and had a lukewarm relationship with God. Then circumstances began to arrange themselves in such a miraculous way that she recognized the hand of God.

1991
The Atlanta Braves were doing well that year and Sandee saw a commercial opportunity.

"I needed to find some little tomahawks (part of the Braves logo) to make earrings, and there weren't any to be found," said Sandee. "I discovered polymer clay and started making them out of that. A whole new world opened up to me."

In learning the properties of polymer clay, Sandee began creative work on little characters she called the "Dimples" dolls. Instead of adding color and patterns with paint, she began to use the colored clay and fabric. The result was enchanting and highly salable.

November 1995
The months leading up to Christmas were Sandee's busiest time with her Dimples characters. She had several big craft shows ahead, but a case of particularly persistent congestion was slowing her down. "I couldn't taste anything, but I ignored that for a while. When I had to do Thanksgiving dinner by memory, I decided it

was time to go see a doctor!" said Sandee.

The doctor's hands moved down Sandee's throat to her lower neck. He thoughtfully palpitated her thyroid. His fingers located a hard little lump, and he had Sandee feel it for herself. "I didn't take it too seriously," said Sandee. "I had never been sick except to have two wisdom teeth removed." But a sonogram image revealed an irregular growth that could either be a benign tumor or cancer. Now Sandee was frightened.

She had never had surgery or anesthesia before. The surgeon told her that surgery could wait until after Christmas, but that the lump and the attached thyroid gland needed to come out.

At the time, Sandee's relationship with God wasn't what it should have been and she wasn't sitting under any Bible teaching. "I knew in the back of my head I wasn't doing what I should be doing," said Sandee.

A neighbor across the street who was a strong Christian believer stood by her and called the prayer room at church to pray for Sandee. "I prayed a little about the date of the surgery, and although I had a big craft show ahead, I decided to go ahead with the surgery," Sandee said.

December 13
While the surgery itself went smoothly, Sandee had a rough time with the anesthetic. "I was panicking and

sick," she said. "I scared my husband because he said I was so white that I was the same color as the sheet!"

The good news was that at first glance, the tumor seemed to be benign. . .but it would be sent away to a lab for analysis. While she waited for the results, Sandee went back to her other activities, never dreaming that her entire life was about to change forever.

When Sandee went back to the surgeon for a check-up, she was greeted with unexpected news: The tumor had been cancerous after all. In fact, it was an aggressive form that had attached itself to the throat muscle. Because it could have metastasized and traveled to other parts of the body, the surgeon recommended that her remaining thyroid gland also be removed. When Sandee no longer had any thyroid hormone in her body, a scan would reveal whether or not the cancer had spread.

So three months after her first surgery, Sandee again had a partial thyroidectomy. Given no synthetic thyroid hormone, Sandee's energy level plummeted and her muscle tone deteriorated. "I basically went from teaching aerobics to being a couch potato against my will. I was always extremely paranoid about my weight. I thought I was fat, even when I was a size six," said Sandee.

But in the six weeks that she waited for her thyroid levels to dip low enough to do the scan, Sandee added forty pounds to her five-foot two-inch frame. While depression is systemic with thyroid problems, it became a major problem for Sandee as she watched her weight increase. Said Sandee: "When I looked in the mirror, I would burst out crying. When I took my daughter shopping, I would pick out something that I thought would fit, but it wouldn't, and I'd start crying in the fitting room. If I ran into someone at the store that I knew from aerobics class, I would hide so they wouldn't see how much weight I'd gained."

While the scan found no evidence of cancer and Sandee was able to start on thyroid replacement therapy, she was unable to return to the aerobics classroom. The operation had permanently left her hoarse and she couldn't make herself heard.

For the first time in ten years, she didn't have an activity on Wednesday. This left her free to go to a Bible study with a friend. "The Bible lessons turned me around," said Sandee, "and eventually helped me understand why all of this had happened to me." Sandee said that she learned that God gives each person a "spiritual gift," a supernatural talent for sharing His love. She also learned that everything you do should be used for God.

"I finally got my spiritual life together and began to think of using my art for God. I tried to think of ways to share Jesus without being preachy, because I never liked that when people did that to me," said Sandee.

Now, she no longer hid when she saw someone from her aerobics class, but looked at it as a way to share her faith. "I'd say, 'I'm heavier than I used to be, but I like myself so much more than I did. I finally got my life figured out,' " she said.

With more time on her hands, Sandee took a doll-making class and began to sculpt art dolls in polymer clay. Small faces started to appear beneath her tools, and ideas flowed out of her mind and took shape in the clay. "During my quiet time with God and Bible study, I began to want to use my talent to witness," said Sandee. It was out of this that her first "witness dolls" began to appear.

Because she had made so many Christmas-theme pieces in the past, she said it was only natural that this series would begin with a Santa doll. Sculpted in polymer clay, Sandee's Santa wearily sits in a chair with his feet up on an ottoman. His coat is off, his suspenders down, he holds a worn Bible which he is raptly reading. In his other hand is a mug of cocoa—complete with miniature "marshmallows." The inscription on the mug reads: "Jesus is the reason for the season." The piece is entitled: "What Christmas Is All About."

The concept for her next piece popped into her head while she read aloud a verse in Sunday school class. This sculpture depicts a young woman holding open a screen door. Down several steps stands a beggar wearing a shabby overcoat and clothing. The title of the piece is a verse, Hebrews 13:2: "Be not forgetful to entertain strangers: for thereby some have entertained angels unawares." Peeking discreetly from beneath the beggar's coat are the tips of his wings.

Sandee said that God used the chain of events miraculously put into motion by His hand to get her attention and to give her an unusual way of testifying to His grace. "If I hadn't had the thyroid problems, I would have kept on doing the aerobics classes. I wouldn't have gone to the Bible study, and I would not have gotten into sculpting," said Sandee. "I would not be witnessing for Him like I am."

Sandee Crockett and her husband, Dale, live in Marietta, Georgia, where Sandee makes her Dimples and art "witness" dolls. She continues to do doll and craft shows. Sandee and Dale have three children and are soon to become grandparents.

$\mathcal{U}$nusual situations sometimes call for unusual messengers. This is what Samson's parents discovered when an angel told them they would have a son and they were to train him from birth to be a deliverer of Israel. The angel gave them a set of instructions on rearing such a child (Judg. 13:1–5).

When Deborah Smith and her family found themselves in unusually difficult circumstances, an angel stopped by to lend a hand and tell her exactly what to do.

SOME ANGELS DRIVE VANS

Like a hopeful pioneer, when Deborah Smith loaded her three children in a station wagon and headed toward the sunset during the summer of 1991, she was looking to begin a new life. The family had passed through many difficult years at the hands of Deborah's former husband, and the experiences had left her and her children edgy and frightened. Deborah was hoping and praying that the month-long vacation across the United States would reestablish her family and heal some of the wounds.

But Deborah and the children were nervous about the trip. Gruesome, graphic details of crimes against children and women had been pounded into them by her ex-husband. In an effort to maintain control over them, he had told them constantly that a woman alone with children was begging to be attacked by mass murderers and violent perverts. Although they lived in a small town with a low crime rate, the children were constantly frightened. Deborah had been praying that God would help them conquer their fears. This trip seemed to be the answer.

Before leaving their campsites as each morning dawned, Deborah and her children, ages six, fourteen, and sixteen, spent time praying and reading the Bible. "First thing, when we hit the road, we would ask for the Lord's protection. Then we'd travel," said Deborah.

Daily, they thrilled to see the constantly changing beauty outside their car windows, from the plains and prairies of the Midwest, to the majestic mountains of Oregon, to the breathtaking California Coastal Highway 101. "It was easy to praise God all the way because of the scenery," said Deborah.

The weather had been perfect and the car had run smoothly until they began to descend the mountains just north of San Francisco and turned east, heading toward Lake Tahoe. The winding two-lane road that led toward the foothills was nearly deserted, with no shoulders or ditches. They traveled miles and miles between intersections or driveways, and they met few other motorists.

Suddenly, steam began rolling off the car hood, and the temperature gauge registered in the red. "I knew we had to stop somewhere along the road," said Deborah.

"It was too far to the next town, so I told the kids, 'Start praying! We need a turnoff.'"

Traveling a scant half a mile farther, they encountered a large roadside rest area. Deborah pulled over and surveyed the scene. There was no telephone, and they were surrounded on all sides by the wooded mountains, with only the thin ribbon of highway connecting them to civilization.

"I thought, *There's nothing here,* and all those old fears planted by my former husband started to come back. This was the nightmare situation we had dreaded." The children were nervous, too, and Deborah wondered what she had been thinking to put them all in jeopardy by taking a road trip.

She lifted the hood of the car and steam billowed out. "Kids," she said, "start praying for protection and help. We're going to have to trust the Lord that He'll keep us safe and get us out."

It wasn't two minutes later that a beat-up van without any business markings pulled over and stopped. A large burly man got out and leaned casually against the grill on the driver's side of his van. "Looks like you got a problem, ma'am," he said in a matter-of-fact tone.

From her position about ten feet away, she looked him over carefully, memorizing his appearance. He seemed to be a working man, and she judged that he stood six feet tall. His fuzzy, reddish-brown hair was clean but unkempt. His shirtsleeves were rolled up, and he was wearing blue jeans.

He watched her closely, seemingly aware that she might be frightened. "Can I take a look?" he asked.

Deborah told the kids to get out of the car and wait for her at the edge of the tree line. She quietly instructed them, "Stand back. If something weird happens, don't wait for me. Duck into the woods and run to safety." Then she nodded to the man.

He took off the radiator cap and they could both see that the antifreeze was gone. "You've got a leak in the radiator hose," he said. "You're out of water. I just returned from a job and I have something that might help you." He returned to his van and pulled out a five-gallon bucket of water with no lid.

Deborah almost laughed out loud. *What kind of person carries around an open five-gallon bucket of water?* she wondered.

He poured the water into the radiator and replaced the lid.

"How far will it get me?" Deborah asked.

"As far as you need to go," he said. "Go down the road and you'll come into a small town. At the intersection, turn right. Go to the second filling station, not the first. I know the owner there and he'll help you."

He got into his van and pulled up to the edge of the highway and waited. As two cars approached, he pulled out in front of them. Deborah watched in astonishment, then called to her children, "Get into the car quickly, kids! This is no coincidence! I think God has just sent us an angel! Keep your eyes on that van!"

Deborah said that the van was just two cars ahead of them as they went around a curve. Past the curve, the highway opened up into a long stretch where they could see for miles. The van and its driver were gone. A silence fell as they realized what had happened. "There were no turnoffs or anything. No exits of any kind," said Deborah, "but he was gone."

Deborah and the children found the service station just as the man described. As the mechanic repaired the hose, Deborah told him, "I really appreciate your friend helping me. It's so refreshing to find honest, considerate people." Then she described her rescuer.

"I don't know who that would be," the mechanic told her. "I don't know anybody who looks like that."

"Maybe the owner of the station does. He said he knew the owner," Deborah told him.

"I am the owner," the mechanic assured her, "and I never knew anybody who looked like that."

As Deborah paid for the repairs and turned to walk away, she thought, *I think there's more to this.* She walked back into the station and said to the owner, "I want to thank you. The Lord's been good to us. You're an answer to prayer."

"Yes," said the mechanic, "He is good. He's my Lord and Savior, too."

Deborah and her children have discussed this miracle many times, and she considers it a turning point in their lives. "This was the epitome of the situation that my former husband said would destroy us, but God looked after us in this, as He would in everything else to come. It was tangible confirmation to us that God was alive and well and would look after us, no matter what anybody said."

Deborah Smith has since married a fine Christian man. She lives with him and her youngest son in Ohio, where she teaches physical education. Her two older children are grown and on their own, but remain close to their mother.

When Noah built his ark, it was a very experimental form of watercraft. No one had ever seen one before. Or needed one. Only Noah and God knew what it was capable of doing (Gen. 6).

When a flood of troubles began to rain down on the Humbarger family, they asked God for wisdom and help, and He provided a custom-made cure.

THE RIGHT MEDICATION

August 1975

Life was great for L.D. and Karen Humbarger. They and their two sons were healthy and happy. Everything was going so well that they decided it was a waste of money to continue paying for major medical insurance. They expected their lives to continue without sickness or trouble —until one day their son Jason was not feeling well.

"We had gone to see *South Pacific* at the Civic Theater and we had a wedding to go to yet that day. But Jason, who was about three at that time, was running a fever," remembered Karen.

Later, she took her son to the doctor. Under the bright lights in the examining room, the doctor pointed out something she hadn't noticed before: little red dots on his legs. The doctor drew blood and sent Karen and

Jason home, but they soon were called to return to the doctor's office.

"You need to come back," the nurse told her. "There's something wrong with Jason's blood." The doctor wanted to do more tests, but he suspected that the little red dots were caused by blood leaking through his veins, a classic symptom of leukemia.

A bone marrow scan and other tests were performed before they heard the chilling diagnosis: acute lymphocytic leukemia. "All we could think about was cancer was a terminal illness and we were going to lose him," Karen remembered. She immediately called a local network of praying Christian believers.

Jason was admitted to Lutheran Hospital, Fort Wayne, Indiana, but the doctors quickly sent him on to St. Jude's in Memphis. "The doctors and staff weren't guaranteeing anything. It is an experimental hospital, and we were told that the kids there were guinea pigs," said Karen. "But we were also told that Jason was at a good age for success. By age three, their bodies are more able to handle the strong medicines required to fight catastrophic diseases."

Jason was immediately put into isolation behind a large plate glass window where no infections or bacteria could get to him. The hospital staff administered medications to enhance his immune system. At the same time he was denied all physical contact with Karen and L.D.: Parents and child were separated by a few centimeters of glass; they could see and talk to one another, but they couldn't touch. So near but so far away, they watched Jason undergo painful tests, but they were unable to comfort him with a soothing touch. "It was very, very hard," said Karen, "but I kept assuring him that this was all needed to make him better."

Once out of isolation, he began radiation and chemotherapy. While most of the kids were very sick following the treatments, Jason did better than expected. "The power of prayer kept him from getting so terribly sick," said Karen. "All the time I was praying, *Please, Lord, let this be the right medicine to put him into remission.*"

Within a few weeks, Jason *was* in remission. "This is the kind of thing God does when we pray," said Karen. "When these things are happening and we don't understand why, it's so important to remember that God is in control."

During the seven weeks Jason was treated at St. Jude's, the hospital personnel, patients, and other parents acted as a surrogate family to the Humbargers. Friendships were forged that would extend during the years following Jason's treatment.

Jason continued to periodically take chemotherapy over the next three years. Normally, treatments take thirty months, but because leukemia was found in more than one area of Jason's body, he was required to continue treatments every Tuesday for thirty-six months.

While on chemotherapy, childhood diseases can become life threatening, so it was imperative to minimize exposure. Many times, Jason's brother Jeff had to be separated from the family to keep Jason from being exposed. Fear of contagion kept the family's nerves stretched until it was almost a relief when Jason finally did get chicken pox. Again, they went back to St. Jude's, where Jason was monitored through a side door especially designated for contagious diseases. However, this was yet another answer to prayer, because Jason recovered with no complications; since both boys finally had the illness, there was less chance that Jeff would have to leave home again.

Karen observed that cancer returned to most of the kids who were with Jason at St. Jude's. She also saw how a catastrophic illness such as cancer not only destroyed the child's health and family, but it broke up marriages and families. "We saw several marriages break up because one member of the family starts to blame the other," said Karen.

Yet the Humbargers were able to weather the storm.

1992

At age seventeen, after ten years off chemotherapy and living cancer-free, Jason noticed an odd lump behind one ear. Immediately, Karen took Jason for examination. Because first reports indicated that it was a benign tumor,

Karen let Jason attend his follow-up doctor's examination alone.

Said Karen: "He called crying. It was a malignant tumor that was attached to every nerve in his face. He would have to have surgery to remove it." Karen immediately called the prayer network, and once again, people got on their knees to pray for Jason's recovery.

The doctors anticipated a one-hour surgery to remove the tumor, but it took more like five hours. Although the tumor was intertwined with all of the nerves on the left side of his face, in the end, he made a full recovery and didn't lose any of the mobility in his face.

Lingering questions remained. Would Jason be able to father children because of the large doses of radiation he received? The specialists at St. Jude didn't know the answer, because so few of their cancer patients lived long enough for that question to become an issue.

Karen prayed that God would inspire the doctors to use the right experimental medication on Jason. Apparently, God answered that prayer.

Jason has been cancer-free since 1992. He and his wife had a baby girl in July 1995 and a son in June 1998.

Karen Humbarger works at Good Humor-Breyers Ice Cream, Huntington, Indiana, and L.D. works for Goeglein Painting and Decorating, Fort Wayne, Indiana. They reside in Markle, Indiana. Jason and his wife Tania and their three children live in Bluffton, Indiana. Jeff is in good health.

Many of the bedrock principles of the Kingdom of heaven—love your enemies, turn the other cheek, do good to those who hate you, etc.— would seem counterproductive if the citizens of the Kingdom weren't counting on the supernatural power of God to work it all out somewhere along the line. Indeed, those principles don't make sense without God.

"Give, it shall be given unto you" (Luke 6:38) is another one of those principles. But anyone who has practiced giving to God knows the miraculous returns. God reserves His best blessings for those who give when they don't have much to give.

MIRACLE IN A WHITE ENVELOPE

On a Sunday morning in 1986, Janelle's ranch-style home hid dark secrets. Although located in a fashionable suburb of a prosperous Indiana city, there was very little food in the cupboard and Janelle had absolutely no money to buy any for her three small children. She knew well that if she asked her husband for grocery money, it would bring down a hail of pointless abuse upon her head, and in the end, he would not give her a dime. This was not a new situation for Janelle, just the continuation of a long, gradually building nightmare.

Nine years earlier, when they were married, "Scott" claimed to be a committed Christian. He was gentle and seemed to be a responsible man with a steady job and plenty of money. But soon after their marriage, Janelle discovered the secret he was hiding behind a generous attitude, a nice car, and fashionable clothing: Scott bought the best of everything until all of his money was gone. Then he borrowed on credit cards to buy additional luxury items.

As their family grew, Scott's spending became increasingly irresponsible. With the pressure of the growing debt, he grew violent toward Janelle, while neglecting both his children and his church. Prior to the birth of their youngest child, Scott quit going to church entirely and began intimidating Janelle with threats, knives, and wildly erratic behavior.

Janelle suspected that her husband, who worked as a paramedic, was still spending everything he earned on items for himself, eating in expensive restaurants, and pursuing other women. She really didn't know how much he earned each week, since he kept that a secret, but she did know that he brought home almost no money. The bills were always past due, and she often had to rely on friends and family for financial help. At the same time, strange women called asking for Scott.

Despite the professional counseling they received, Janelle suspected her marriage would soon end. But today, feeding the kids weighed more heavily on her mind. As she anxiously searched the refrigerator and cupboards, she realized how desperate the food situation had become. There was not a can of any sort in the cupboard. No bread, no cereal—nothing. At last, she found a small amount of flour, a little shortening, and a splash of milk. Using a bit of ingenuity and the sparse ingredients, Janelle stirred together biscuits.

Janelle said that in those dark days, she often thought of Isaiah 54, where God promises to be husband and protector to those afflicted and lashed by trouble. She mixed up the biscuits while silently telling the Lord, *You know this is all I have for my children. It is up to You to provide for us.*

Noisy, happy, and unaware that this might be their last meal for a while, the three children ate the small batch of biscuits while Janelle watched. "I don't remember that I ate anything," said Janelle. "I do remember that I offered my share to the Lord as a sacrifice, but there wasn't anything left over."

They drove from the suburbs to their inner-city church, where a lively group of believers worshipped. Janelle said a woman whom she barely knew met her at the back of the church and handed her a small, white envelope. "This is not from me," the woman told her. "I was asked to give it to you."

Opening it, Janelle found $40 in cash. "Who is it from?" Janelle asked.

"It is an anonymous gift," the woman said, refusing to divulge even a hint of whom the benefactor might be. Janelle believes it was a gift from God.

Since her divorce from Scott and reentry into the

workforce, Janelle has seen God take care of their needs in miraculous ways time and time again. "I've walked with the Lord since I was seventeen. Watching how He provides is just a part of the adventure of knowing Christ."

Janelle still lives in the ranch-style house in the suburbs with her youngest son.

Many people who doubt that heaven is an actual place hope that hell is not. God, who wants no one to perish, probably wishes hell were not real, too.

While there are many examples in the Bible of people who have come back to life because of prayer, nothing is recorded concerning what they saw or experienced while they were dead. But in His parables, Jesus warned the unrepentant that they should expect utter darkness, weeping, and gnashing of teeth (Matt. 8:12), unquenchable fire (Matt. 3:12), the company of Satan and his minions (Rev. 20:10), and eternal separation from God (Matt. 25:41).

Bill Anderson didn't believe hell existed until he went there—and the prayers of believers and the grace of God pulled him back from hell's brink for a second chance.

Salvation at Hell's Front Door

"Seeing is believing," was Bill Anderson's creed. If he didn't see it with his own eyes, he simply didn't believe it. This hard-nosed attitude extended to God. Bill couldn't see Him. Therefore, He did not exist.

On numerous occasions during the ten years she had been a believer in Christ, his daughter Eve Padilla talked with Bill about his soul. "He had too many unanswered questions about God and the Bible," said Eve. "He was a wonderful father and a good man, but he'd give me a hard time when I tried to talk with him about God." Each time, he maneuvered her into the same corner from which she couldn't escape: Bill couldn't see God. Therefore, God did not exist.

Then in April 1995, at age sixty-three, Bill Anderson developed a severe case of diabetes and a sore on his

left foot. By the time he sought medical care, he had tox-
ins throughout his body, leaving the doctors no choice but
to amputate the foot.

His diabetic condition worsened. In the next three
years, Bill underwent three subsequent amputations and a
total of seven operations. As the only Christian believer in
her family, Eve often prayed for her father's salvation.
Then God answered her prayer in an unexpected way.

Trinity Hospital
Moline, Illinois
Summer 1995
The first time Eve ever saw her father cry was when
doctors told him that his right leg must now be ampu-
tated, too. "His condition was really bad," said Eve.
"The doctors told us that he had to have the amputation
to live, but that he was so bad he might not make it
through surgery."

She knew it would be sad if he died, but a tragedy if
he perished without Christ. It was at this life-or-death
moment that Eve summoned prayer warriors. "There is
a ladies' prayer chain in town," said Eve, "made up of
women from all different churches. I explained the situation to the leader and asked them all to pray. What I
didn't know until later was that they agreed together in
prayer that Dad wouldn't die unless he was assured of
going to heaven." That prayer would become the pivotal
point in Bill Anderson's eternal future.

The amputation was a long, five- to six-hour surgery. Hours dragged and tension remained high as Eve waited outside the operating room with her four sisters and one brother. Finally, someone suggested that they go outside while they continued to wait.

The day was uncomfortably hot as the family sat in the sunshine wondering whether their father would live or die. Eve asked her brother and sisters if they would pray with her that their father would pull through. Although they were not believers, the six siblings bowed their heads as Eve prayed aloud.

"Suddenly, a wonderful, cool breeze began to blow," said Eve. "It sounds strange, but I felt as though it blew through me, refreshing me and building me up." In the breeze, the Lord spoke to Eve, assuring her that her father would live through the operation. Uplifted, she told her sisters and brother what God said to her.

"Oh, really? That's good," was their response. At that tense moment, Eve thought perhaps this word from the Lord would give them some encouragement, and it seemed to. But their elation was short lived. After they went back to the waiting room, a nurse greeted them with very bad news.

"Your dad died on the operating table," she told them solemnly, "but we were able to revive him. You need to see him now because he isn't going to be alive very much longer."

All eyes turned to Eve. "I thought Dad was going to

be okay!" someone said. "Are you sure you heard right?" Eve felt very alone, but she clung to the peace God had given her.

Although he was now missing both legs and attached to a labyrinth of tubes, to Eve, Bill Anderson still appeared to be the big, stocky man he always had been—until he opened his eyes and looked directly into Eve's. "He was speaking to me through his eyes," said Eve. "Instantly, I knew what had happened."

A tube in his throat inhibited his speech, but he made motions that he wanted to write. In a ragged but readable script, he penned, "If I make it through this, there will be major changes in my life."

"Dad, did you die?" Eve asked him.

Although he burst into anguished tears, his eyes remained open wide with fright. He nodded.

"Did you see heaven?"

Slowly, looking only at Eve, he shook his head.

"Did you see hell?"

Alarm buzzers began to scream. Bill nodded emphatically, sobs tearing at his chest.

Reaching through the tubes and wires, Eve put her arms around her father while the rest of the family looked on. "God told me that you wouldn't die now. Please believe that," she pleaded with him.

By the next morning, to everyone's surprise, Bill's condition had stabilized and they were able to remove the respirator. Although still in the intensive care unit, he was waiting anxiously for his family to arrive. He had something to say.

Weak, but sitting upright in bed, Bill told his children about his death only the day before. He described how he had floated above the doctors and saw his own legless body, lying lifeless on the operating table. However, he noted, his spiritual body had two legs.

He tried to tap the surgeon's shoulder, but to his surprise and frustration, his hand went through the man's body. As the realization dawned that he was dead, his soul quickly moved into a long, dark tunnel. Two beings appeared on either side, holding his arms as they escorted him down the corridor.

"Wait a minute!" he cried. "What's going on here?"

The beings didn't speak, but a terror he had never known on earth enveloped him. He was afraid to look at his silent escorts, but horrible evil emanated from them and a sense of dread gripped him.

Suddenly, the corridor ended. Bill and the two beings stood before a door. Automatically, it opened. Before him lay total darkness. Terrible, anguished cries belched forth. Then the beings began to shove him over the threshold into the abyss.

"I'm not going in!" Bill told them, desperately struggling to escape their grasp and run from the darkness.

One of the beings spoke: "Bill, this is the only place

you have to go. This was your choice." That was the last he remembered until he saw Eve's face.

"Now do you know what I've been telling you is true?" asked Eve. "Are you ready to accept Christ?" While her unbelieving family looked on, Eve prayed a simple sinner's prayer with Bill.

For the next years of his life, Bill told his story to many with whom he came into contact.

He did not go to be with the Lord until four years later on November 18, 1998.

Postscript

Bill Anderson often said that he believed God allowed him to see hell because of his "I-have-to-see-it-to-believe-it" attitude. "I know if there is one side—hell—there has to be another—heaven," he told Eve.

At first, his other children thought Bill's vision of hell was a hallucination. But as he persisted in his belief in Christ and began to ask forgiveness of people whom he felt he had wronged, they knew he had had a life-changing experience. To date, Eve is still the only surviving member of her family to believe in Christ, but some are starting to rethink this because of their father's experience.

Bill frequently commented that he believed his illness was brought on by his constant rejection of Christ. However, when he anguished over the loss of his legs,

Eve reminded him that it was far better for him to have lost his legs than his soul.

On Labor Day weekend 1998, prior to Bill's death, Eve and her father made a pact. "When you die, if there is any way at all that God will allow you, will you give me a sign that you are in heaven?" Eve asked.

Bill agreed and they shook on it.

The day after Bill died, Eve recalled that she heard a continual whisper urging her to "look into the sky." She stepped outside of her farmhouse and saw what looked like a huge golden-orange spotlight shining down on her. "It was the most vibrant color I've ever seen!" said Eve. The source of the light was also golden orange and spinning, with bits of fire swirling off it, painting the sky with beautiful color.

"I'm looking at this, wondering, *What is going on here?* Then it hit me. This was my sign. It was not what I was expecting, but I realized now that God loved me so much that He let my father—and me—see His light. I thank God for His compassion. He gave me the sign I needed."

Bill Anderson was a retired machinist from John Deere.

Eve Anderson Padilla is married with three sons and works as a real estate agent.

God sometimes requires us to be persistent in prayer.

A Canaanite woman—commonly thought to be a member of a heathen nation—doggedly followed Jesus and his disciples until the disciples began to complain, "Jesus! Send her away!" But the Canaanite woman persevered in prayer until she received an answer: Jesus indeed healed her daughter (Matt. 15:21–28).

Sometimes God tests our resolve. Do we really believe in His ability to heal? Will we continue to trust in His goodness if He says "No"? Are we willing to ask and ask and ask?

When a young woman in his congregation fell ill, a pastor and his wife besieged the throne of God until they knew their prayers had been heard.

A Cure for Polio

Nearly every summer during the first half of the twentieth century, mothers all over the United States held their
breath until after the first hard frost. Polio was an illness
that stuck terror into their hearts, and after the frost,
instances usually declined. There was no known way to
prevent this crippling disease because no one actually
knew how it was passed from one person to the next. A
frightfully mysterious plague, for all anyone knew, it could
be spread by any means. The only thing for mothers to do
was scald the dishes, thoroughly cook all foods, and keep
their children out of farm ponds and swimming holes. But
once contracted, everyone knew the result: The victim
could be left slightly paralyzed. . .or mentally and physically crippled. . .or dead.

Fairy Brunner Derrer credits the power of prayer

for her survival and complete recovery from this dread affliction.

Sunday, November 15, 1945
Lanark, Illinois

For about a week, fourteen-year-old Fairy Brunner had been dragging through her school days with flu-like symptoms. As the weekend approached, she thought she could rest and soon feel better. But she felt worse on Saturday, and by Sunday, she had difficulty swallowing.

Her mother called Dr. Petty, the family physician, and described the symptoms of her only child. He prepared some medicine for her, and Mrs. Brunner went down to his office to pick it up. "If she's not better by morning, call me," Dr. Petty instructed.

Monday, November 16, 1945

By morning, Fairy was burning with fever. Her eyes would no longer focus properly, and she could not swallow.

When Dr. Petty was summoned to the house, he carefully examined Fairy. He was suspicious that she might have contracted polio, but he knew his guesses would need to be confirmed by a hospital test.

"Whatcha doing, kid?" he asked her.

"Taking a vacation," she told him.

"I think you better take a long one." He advised her parents to take her to Freeport Memorial Hospital in

Freeport, Illinois, for a spinal tap.

A spinal tap confirmed the country doctor's diagnosis, but by that time, Fairy's condition had worsened and she appeared to have lost consciousness. As unresponsive as she was, though, she could still hear what was being said about her.

"She has *bulbar polio*," the Freeport physician told Mrs. Brunner. "Only about 5 percent of patients who contract this survive."

Upon hearing the doctor's gloomy forecast, Fairy wondered if she would live or die. But she felt calm and unafraid. "Whether it was my Christian faith that I would be in heaven with Jesus that kept me calm or the illness itself dulling my emotions, I'm not sure," said Fairy. "For one reason or another, I just accepted the statement and wondered whether I would be in the 5 percent or the 95 percent."

Since the Freeport hospital had no other cases of polio, they didn't want Fairy contaminating the wards. An ambulance raced the critically ill Fairy to Winnebago County Hospital in Rockford, Illinois. Winnebago was filled with mostly elderly patients, but since they also housed a small population of polio patients there, they agreed to take Fairy.

Fairy floated in and out of consciousness as the ambulance transported her to Rockford. She wondered if this was not only her first ambulance ride, but also her last.

The Brunner Farm
Lanark, Illinois
Tuesday, November 17, 1945
4 A.M.

A shrill telephone ring awoke Mr. and Mrs. Brunner in the wee morning hours. On the line was Winnebago County Hospital, where Fairy was still a patient. "Your daughter is critically ill," Mrs. Brunner was told, "and she may not survive long enough for you to come to the hospital." When Mrs. Brunner related the message to her husband, he fainted on the spot.

A woman of action, Mrs. Brunner telephoned the family's pastor and asked him to pray. Then she called Dr. Petty, requesting that he drive them the sixty-five miles to Rockford.

The Brunners' car—a 1929 Pontiac—wouldn't have made it. But Dr. Petty had a better car than they did, and he drove faster than anyone in Carroll County. Doctors at that time were more like family friends—and they were the only ones not afraid of polio.

The Parsonage
Lanark, Illinois
Tuesday, November 17, 1945
4 A.M.

The Brunners' telephone call stirred the pastor and his wife into action. Fairy was a young woman who was dear to them, and she was also the church pianist. They dropped to their knees and began to pray fervently for Fairy's recovery.

Winnebago County Hospital
Rockford, Illinois
Tuesday, November 17, 1945
4 A.M.

After the phone call to summon Fairy's parents, the doctors and staff went back to work trying to stabilize her condition. Her pulse was erratic and her breathing labored.

Suddenly, her breathing stopped. Doctors listened in vain for a heartbeat. There was nothing more they could do. The doctors and nurses looked helplessly at one another. It is always a solemn moment for health-care professionals when they wrestle with death and lose, but never more so than when the arena is a young person. Now, they had decisively lost the bout. There remained nothing more for them to do but to pull the sheet over her head and declare defeat.

The Parsonage
Lanark, Illinois
Tuesday, November 17, 1945
Sometime after 4 A.M.

Still on their knees beseeching the Great Physician to

heal Fairy, the pastor and his wife suddenly received a peaceful sensation of assurance in their souls. Their prayers had been heard. The crisis was over. Rejoicing, they glanced at their watches and went back to bed.

Winnebago County Hospital
Rockford, Illinois
Tuesday, November 17, 1945
Sometime after 4 A.M.

As the doctors and nurses took one final glance at Fairy's still body, they noticed something unexpected: Her color had returned and she was breathing. They hurriedly checked her pulse and found that it had returned.

Mr. and Mrs. Brunner, shepherded by Dr. Petty, arrived at the hospital moments later. The doctors and nurses were still shaking their heads over what they had witnessed. "Fairy stopped breathing and had no pulse, but something happened that we cannot explain in medical terms," they told the Brunners. "She is alive and it is nothing we did, but a miracle from the hand of a Higher Power than ours."

"What time did this happen?" Mrs. Brunner asked.

Later, she would discover that the time corresponded precisely with the minute the pastor and his wife knew God had answered their prayers.

Fairy was still alive, but the news was not entirely good.

The hospital personnel told Mr. and Mrs. Brunner that they were uncertain if she would still continue to recover. Most likely, if she did live, she would not have normal intelligence, her memory would be lost, and her eyes would neither look normal in appearance nor would she have vision. While the Brunners desperately wanted Fairy to live, they did not want her to be so terribly handicapped.

Late January 1946
Despite all of the gloomy predictions, Fairy made steady progress until she was released from the hospital two or three weeks after she first regained her ability to swallow. Each day, she was permitted to be out of bed for a few minutes longer.

On her second or third day home from the hospital, she sat down at the piano, and partly from memory and partly by sight-reading the music, she played a thirty-two-page classical selection she had been memorizing before she became ill. "My mother cried with joy as she watched me play," said Fairy. "My parents and I continued to praise the Lord. We're always glad for the opportunity to relate the story of my miraculous survival and recovery."

Postscript
Fairy's was an isolated case of polio in the county and none of her schoolmates contracted it.

In March 1946, she was able to return to school for half days. With the help of teachers and a lot of homework, she was able to catch up with her class. The following term, she was promoted.

Mrs. Brunner died a few years after Fairy's illness, and Fairy assumed the care of her father. When she married Wayne Derrer, he joined Fairy and her father on the farm. They farmed for thirty-nine years until Wayne retired. He now is a maintenance man for a handicapped workshop. Fairy is still organist at her local church. Fairy and Wayne Derrer have two children and five grandchildren and still reside near Lanark.

*I*n a fashion that was both amusing and miraculous, God provided protection for Elisha and his servant when the king of Aram threw all of his resources into capturing Elisha (2 Kings 6:8–23). God struck the soldiers blind and then led the hunters on a wild, fruitless chase.

At one time, the press mercilessly harassed Donna Rice Hughes. Reporters wanted to question her about a suspected affair with a presidential candidate. When she refused their interview requests, they retaliated by destroying her reputation with innuendo. Now, years later, she had a sexually sensitive cause to promote. What would the press do to her now?

Hidden in Plain Sight

In 1987, Donna Rice Hughes found herself in the midst of a national scandal. Once the story broke, the worldwide press hounded her mercilessly, in many instances inventing "facts" and salacious rumors to fill pages and broadcasts. As she was held up to public ridicule, her family was also humiliated. But a mere five years later, in a miraculous way, God rehabilitated both her name and image by placing her in a very public forum while temporarily blinding the eyes of would-be critics to her identity. In the process, He also brought healing to her parents.

May 4, 1987
As the front-running Democratic candidate for president, Colorado senator Gary Hart was besieged by rumors of womanizing. While denying the stories, he

foolishly challenged reporters, "Follow me." They did. This led them to Hart's Washington D.C. townhouse. Five *Miami Herald* reporters staked it out.

On Friday, at 11 P.M., when the reporters knew that Hart's wife was out of town, they saw a young woman enter his townhouse. She left on Saturday morning at about 8:30 A.M. That woman was Donna Rice. Although Hart vehemently denounced their report as "character assassination," the circumstances were indeed incriminating, and the press was titillated by the possibilities.

When Donna read the news story, she begged the Hart campaign to keep secret her identity. But through some mysterious means, she was identified and found herself the object of intense press curiosity. Shortly after that, Hart withdrew his candidacy because of the threatened exposure of his questionable relationship with another young woman.

A few days later, *The National Inquirer* broke a story, complete with photos, relating that Donna and Hart had taken a cruise together. But the trauma was still not over for Donna. For the next year and a half, her reputation was smeared all over the world by false and faulty news reports.

At first, the stories were flattering. But when Donna refused to be interviewed on the details of her relationship with Hart, the coverage turned ugly. Starved for details, the news sharks began to circle. Although

Donna had a promising career and had graduated from college magna cum laude, news reports characterized her as a "prostitute" and party girl. Horrified, Donna naively still believed the truth would soon emerge.

Said Donna: "I thought, *I'm not going to take this seriously. If I just be who I am, people won't believe all of this.* But when the stories continued, the press's perception began to penetrate the public's perception. It became very painful. Then I thought, *How can this happen? How can these people who don't know me say these things?*"

Even her family was not exempt from the media's distortions. A quote from her father was twisted to sound like an indictment against her.

While other people who make public mistakes escape with little ridicule and scrutiny, the media was going for her jugular. However, she does not regret the experience. "God was calling me back to Himself. I fell on my knees before Him. It had taken an international scandal to get my attention," she said.

This was the beginning of a seven-year restoration process. During this time, Donna said she took baby steps back to God.

May 1994
After Donna began working for the antipornographic organization, Enough Is Enough, in Fairfax, Virginia, she became highly concerned about the availability of

Internet pornography to children. Perceiving this new frontier of perversion to be filled with insidious dangers, she brought the matter to the attention of Dee Jepsen, president of Enough Is Enough. Encouraged by Dee to investigate the pervasiveness of cyberporn and come up with some ideas on how to stem it, Donna then fed the information to Dee in preparation for a presentation in the Congressional Caucus Room in Washington, D.C.

June 1995

Time was drawing near for Enough Is Enough's presentation. It would be given to members of Congress and the entire media corps. Donna assumed Dee would be the spokesperson, but instead she turned to Donna.

"You know more about it than anyone," Dee told her. "This is your subject." But Donna was reluctant to add her name to the issue. She liked the anonymity she now enjoyed, so she made it a matter for prayer. "This is a sexually stigmatized issue, Lord. You've got to be kidding!" Although she didn't understand God's reasoning, as she prayed, she felt that God wanted her to come out of hiding and make the presentation.

Her parents, hoping to protect Donna from another onslaught of lies, encouraged her to drop the "Rice" from her name and use only her first name and married name: Donna Hughes. But Donna felt God was leading her a different way.

"The world's perception of me is from five years ago," she told her parents, "and it will never be changed unless I stand up. I have to do what God is calling me to do."

As Donna Rice Hughes, she made her presentation in the Congressional Caucus Room. Television cameras rolled and newspaper photographers snapped shots. One of those photographs showed Donna sitting with another presidential candidate. This time, it was Republican hopeful Robert Dole, but not one reporter noticed the irony of it—because no one recognized Donna as a part of the 1987 scandal. God hid her in plain sight before the American press, the eyes and ears of the world.

Microphones were shoved under her nose and questions were posed. Reporters queried her on numerous sexually sensitive subjects. But it wasn't until after she gave her first few hundred interviews and established herself as a spokeswoman for decency that anyone made the connection between Donna Rice Hughes of Enough Is Enough and Donna Rice of the 1987 Gary Hart presidential bid. Finally, the *New York Times* did a huge article about Donna and her work to promote Internet safety.

Soon the media was asking senators and their mates, "What's it like working with Donna Rice?"

"Donna Rice? We don't know Donna Rice. We never knew her," they responded nervously. They did admit to knowing Donna Rice Hughes, a credible, articulate, intelligent, and knowledgeable lobbyist—but she certainly could not be the infamous party girl.

"By preserving my anonymity at first, the Lord gave me a remarkable window of time to get my feet wet," said Donna.

Because Donna was now granting interviews, reporters had opportunity to ask the questions that they had panted to ask back in 1987; however, that was old news and the novelty soon wore off. The story of the day was that Donna and Enough Is Enough were making historic strides in protecting children from Internet pornography. Eventually, she was instrumental in helping to pass the Communications Decency Act.

Occasionally, however, her past relationship with Hart still is mentioned, but it no longer is a problem for Donna. "It doesn't matter when people ask me about it," she said. "Life has gone on and God is using it in a public way. It's part of who I am and what has made me up.

"What has been harder is for people around me to have to re-experience the 1987 scandal. But over time, my parents have come to be blessed, because they see me making a difference and now they can let go of their anger and hurt. They've seen God work with the public platform I have to protect kids on the Internet. Whenever they see me on television, they say, 'I'm so proud of you.'

"It is absolutely ironic, but I am God's evidence of what He can do with a destroyed life. I was held up as the example of what not to do in the area of morality. Now I am being called on regularly to speak to issues of morality. It is the embarrassing things in our lives that He uses to minister to other people."

As vice president of marketing and public relations for Enough Is Enough, Donna has given over one thousand interviews on the need to protect children on the Internet. She has written one book on the subject, Protecting Your Children in Cyberspace *(Baker Book House) and is writing a second. She and her husband, Jack Hughes, jointly own and operate Phoenix Financial and Advisory Service. They live in northern Virginia.*

*A*bout the time His disciples thought they were very wise and important, Jesus sat one of those grubby little people with a runny nose who is constantly asking questions in the middle of them. Then He told them they needed to humble themselves like this child if they were to please God (Matt. 18:1–6). Over and over again, God uses the weak to conquer the strong and the foolish to confound the wise—just to demonstrate to everyone who is paying attention that, in our weakness, God's strength is made perfect (1 Cor. 1:20–25).

In this story, the Heindel family seemed encumbered with children. Many observers doubted if a family with five children could be effective as missionaries. But God chose them specifically to reach a Russian city for the gospel.

FIVE LITTLE SECRET WEAPONS

The Russian minister of education stood before a gathering of the Organization of Christian Schools International and announced, "For seventy years we have shut God out of our society and we see that this did not work. We want you to come and teach us about the Bible." For nearly seventy years, Christian believers all over the globe had been praying for this moment, yet it was barely covered by the world press.

No one knew how long this window of opportunity would remain open, but the consensus was that time was of the essence. Across denominational lines, a call was sent for Christians to spend a year in Russia instructing teachers about the Bible, so that they could in turn instruct their students.

Neptune, Ohio
Early Spring 1995

As Keith and Crista Heindel turned over the garden soil behind their home for planting, they knew God was preparing their lives for a major change. Said Crista: "There was this restlessness that God had something for us to do. He had planted in our hearts that we should begin looking for an open door."

Their lives were already complicated and uncertain. As parents of five children, Crista schooled the three oldest at home and cared for the two younger ones while she and Keith remodeled their aged farmhouse. Rumors were circulating in the community that the local bicycle factory where Keith worked might be closing. They didn't know where God wanted them to go or what He wanted them to do, but they began to pray for guidance and waited.

July 1995
Missionary Church General Conference
Heritage Village, North Carolina

Although Keith's nephew, Brian Heindel, had been diagnosed with a brain tumor, he accompanied Associate Pastor Bill Reith to their denomination's annual gathering of preachers, missionaries, and delegates. Newly graduated from Bible college with a degree in pastoral ministries, Brian had a burning desire to share the gospel, even though he already knew his young life would be cut short. From his wheelchair, Brian heard one of the keynote speakers relate the challenge of the Russian minister of education.

"The doors are wide open now," the speaker told the convention, and he issued a call for one hundred people from the denomination to commit to going to Russia. While Brian knew that he couldn't go to Russia, he prayed that God would send someone in his place. He never suspected that God would send his uncle, aunt, and five cousins.

While he prayed, a pastor came to the front of the auditorium. Weeping with joy at the open door to Russia, he announced, "My church is at such a place that I cannot go to Russia myself. But I'm going to go back to my church committed to raising up people who can go."

Pastor Bill Reith felt God wanted him to take his wife and sons to Russia, but he planned to follow this pastor's example and encourage others in his home church to join him, too. He knew that Keith and Crista were looking for a ministry opportunity, so as soon as he returned home, he said to them, "I have to talk to you about Russia."

A short time later while they enjoyed a local festival parade whose route stretched in front of Bill's house, he told Keith about the invitation issued by the Russian education minister. Crista heard bits and pieces of what

Bill said, but her concentration was scattered as she cared for their youngest child, who had developed a bad case of diarrhea.

"I was running back and forth from the house to the yard trying to listen to what Bill was saying and changing Abram's diapers, so I didn't get to hear most of it," said Crista. "But when we were in the car, I looked over at Keith and said, 'What did Bill say?' Keith had tears in his eyes. He was all choked up and couldn't talk."

That was a watershed point in their lives. "We both knew that Russia was where we were going."

End of September 1995

The more Keith and Crista prayed about taking their family to Russia, the more they were convinced that this was what God wanted. They were accepted by OMS International and were sent to Greenwood, Indiana, for training. It was there that they began to explore the amount of money it would take to send and support them. Since the organization had never sent a family of seven, many variables had to be considered.

At first, they were told that since it cost $42,000 a year for a family of two to go, it might run as high as $50,000 for the entire family. "But they kept upping the dollar amount," said Crista. "Every time we talked to them, it was $10,000 more."

Meanwhile, Keith and Crista began soliciting money

to support their trip. Said Crista: "We started our fundraising the first of October. When we presented our vision to the local church, they were 100 percent behind us."

Finally, OMS International reached a definitive amount. Keith and Crista would need about $83,000 in pledged support. This seemed like an unreachable sum to the Heindels. "We lived frugally and still do," said Crista. "At that point, I thought, *That's three or four times my husband's salary for a year! I think the Lord just wants to know if we are willing to go. He's not really going to require us to go!*"

Many people also doubted the wisdom of sending a family of seven to Russia. Crista was accosted by a lady at church who informed her, "If you think we're going to pay for you to go on a vacation to Russia, you've got another thing coming!"

The Heindels went from home to home and talked with friends about the amount needed. Soon pledges of support began to come in the mail. Ever the teacher, Crista secured a large map to the wall, and for every $2,000 that came in pledges, stars were affixed to span the distance from Ohio to Russia.

In nine weeks' time, at a pace of more than $9,000 a week, their goal was reached. OMS International told the Heindels to stop counting money and start packing their suitcases.

January 1996
Rybinsk, Russia

"Our purpose there was to teach a school curriculum, 'Christian Ethics and Morality: A Foundation for Society'," said Crista. "We were to teach this to school teachers who would, in turn, teach their students."

While this program had been effective in other Russian cities, in Rybinsk, however, they did not have much success getting into schools. Keith and Crista decided to conduct home Bible studies and form English clubs with the purpose of teaching the language with the Bible as the textbook. "There was such a hunger in the people," said Crista. "They were enthusiastic to learn about the Bible.

"The Russians are an intelligent people and voracious readers. As we moved along through the year, we transitioned by turning the Bible studies and English clubs over to the Russian nationals in preparation for when we would leave the city."

While many had thought their large family would be a detriment to their effectiveness, the Russians of Rybinsk were fascinated by this big American family who had come to their city. "There was no traveling incognito," said Crista. "We stood out."

She said that the typical Russian woman will have six to eight abortions in her married life, because they have no form of contraception and can only afford very small families. But despite all of that, the Russian people revere children, saying, "They are our future."

A visionary person had told the Heindels, "Your children will likely open doors of ministry for your family"—and this proved to be the case. Their children made friends with kids of all ages. These youngsters and their families came to the Heindel home and heard about the gospel.

"There is a church in Rybinsk now," said Crista, "and when we hear reports from missionaries, the young families who are coming to the church say, 'We are here because of the Heindels' children.'"

⚜

While the Heindel family has returned to Ohio, Keith plans to return to Russia with a work team to build a bathhouse for a camp. Their oldest son, Aaron, age seventeen, also plans to return to Russia to help in an English camp where Russians come to learn the language and the Bible. Crista is dabbling in a home business while directing the adult and children choirs at her church, home-schooling their children, and caring for a huge garden.

The temple tax was not a mere social obliga-tion; it was an important indication of a man's loyalty to God. And it was expensive, amounting to about two days' wages. When the collectors of the two-drachma tax came to Peter and asked, "Doesn't your teacher pay the temple tax?" the questioner clearly had a malicious intent. If the Jewish leaders could discredit Jesus in any way, they certainly want-ed to do it!

But Jesus was careful not to offend them. He told Peter to throw a line in the lake. Peter was to look inside the mouth of the first fish he caught—and he would find enough money to pay the temple tax for both himself and Jesus.

Bekah Montgomery's situation was a little differ-ent. She wanted to make a good first impression on a newly joined social club, but she found herself in a ridiculous predicament that required divine interven-tion. But just as Jesus provided a miraculous answer to Peter's situation, God also bailed out Bekah.

THE TEACUPS ON A THOUSAND SHELVES

Bekah's situation all began with noble intentions, but it had turned into such a "Lucy and Ethel episode" that she was almost embarrassed to pray about it.

"My family was new in town; in a foolish move to get acquainted and be hospitable, I agreed to hostess a tea in my home for an upper-crust ladies' club. When I volunteered, it didn't seem like a big deal. After all, in the past I had easily catered sit-down dinners for seventy-five to one hundred people. *This should be a piece of cake,* I thought—with tea or coffee to go with the cake," said Bekah.

In her imagination, she set the table with nice paper plates, coordinated paper napkins, petits fours, mints, and so on. Too late she realized that the ladies of the club were accustomed to having their crumpets served on genuine china. Even then, she wasn't too concerned.

"As a part-time antique dealer, I figured I would come across a suitable tea service well before the party. Searching for it would be part of the fun!" said Bekah.

She did own a small tea service, a gift from her late mother-in-law that had been added to by her sister. The pattern was a common one from the 1940s called "moss rose," and Bekah had seen numerous pieces of it here and there. *No problem*, thought Bekah. *It will be a small matter to buy up enough odd bits to competently serve the ladies. When the tea is over, I will sell off the excess and keep my original set.*

So wrong! Whereas once upon a time, she had found pieces of moss rose china everywhere, now that she was diligently seeking them, they fled before her as if she were the proverbial bull bent on their destruction. She searched vainly at antique malls, auctions, garage sales, flea markets—and found only a few stray pieces, most prohibitively priced. As the tea grew closer, she was starting to get panicky. The tea party loomed over her like a tornado inexorably heading her way.

Her lack of china was still weighing on Bekah one sunny Saturday morning as she was running errands all over the countryside. The ditches were fairly blooming with rummage sale signs pointing every which way. And antique auction signs, too. Any other day, she would have been delighted, but she was in a severe time crunch just then. She simply didn't have time to meander all over searching for the elusive moss rose teacup. Somewhere out there in Junkland a full set was blooming brightly for her, but where?

"Lord," Bekah prayed aloud in her car, "You know where there is enough moss rose dishes to serve this tea. I wish You'd just put a golden arrow over that particular sale so I could find it. If You would just show me where to go. . ." Bekah babbled on and on to God, feeling very foolish about bothering Him with teacups and such folderol. After all, there were little children going hungry and she was whining to God about teacups!

However, as she prayed, she felt the Lord nudging her to follow the first garage sale sign in the next little town she encountered. Bekah said she laughed out loud at the sheer ridiculousness of it all, but her heart was light with anticipation. Singing loudly in her car as she bounced up and down over the Illinois prairie, she composed new words to the old song, "He Owns the Cattle on a Thousand Hills."

"He owns the teacups on a thousand shelves," Bekah sang, "the plates in every cupboard!"

Pulling into the next little burg, Bekah could scarcely believe her eyes. There was her golden arrow. It was cardboard, but it was gold, and printed on it were the words "Garage Sale." Bekah thought to herself, *Surely my teacups will be at the end of the arrow!*

The arrow pointed toward a rundown area of town, but she followed it, knowing full well that it was an unlikely spot for antique treasure. However, her heart truly sank when she saw a second golden arrow indicating a jumbled yard full of rickety sawhorses supporting sheets of plywood. Their tops were piled full of whatnots with a few antiques thrown in.

She got out of the car and scanned the assortment of greasy margarine tubs, balls of florescent yarn, and old magazines. No tea set. *Well*, she thought disappointedly, *golden arrows or not, I heard God wrong.*

But the Voice in her heart urged again, *Ask! Ask!*

Reluctantly, she kicked her way through the yard litter and dog bones and approached the lady of the house. As she described the china pattern she was looking for, the woman began to regard her oddly.

"I have a tea set that sounds sorta like that and I want to sell it," she told Bekah. "I didn't put it out because I was waiting for the right person."

She went into her house and returned with a teacup, saucer, and a few other assorted pieces. "Is this what you're looking for?" she asked.

It was the moss rose pattern. She had a goodly number of cups and dessert plates, plus some unusual pieces, and they agreed on a price for all of it. Marveling at God's sense of humor and goodness, Bekah took them home, washed them, and put them in her china cupboard to await the tea.

She was still one cup short, but did it matter? No doubt God knew in advance that one lady was not coming. She decided to put God in charge of attendance.

He had already done a terrific job on the table service committee!

A few days later, as Bekah and a friend ate lunch downtown, she told her friend about the tea set and how God had provided. They laughed together about the preposterousness of the situation, but they rejoiced in God's goodness and supernatural sense of humor. As they walked out of the restaurant door still laughing, they both stopped short. From a distance, they could see that there was something on the hood of Bekah's car, winking in the sunlight. Staring, they recognized it at the same moment.

It was a moss rose teacup! Where it came from Bekah still does not know. She has grilled numerous people she thought might be culpable, but everyone denies any knowledge of the cup. "I know this story will seem like a fairy tale to many," said Bekah, "and if it hadn't happened to me, I would have thought so, too. But I can only draw one conclusion: God does indeed own the teacups on a thousand shelves—and He knows where every one of them is, too!"

Bekah Montgomery is a marketing consultant specializing in downtown revitalization as well as a part-time antique dealer. She and her husband John have three children and live in Illinois.

$\mathcal{W}$hen God told Abraham to leave the cosmopolitan town of Ur of the Chaldeans and "go to a land I will show you" (Gen. 12:1), no doubt Abraham encountered some resistance from friends and family. After all, his move seemed like a foolhardy thing to do. And when Abraham and Sarah reached the new land, they found a severe famine. Had they made a mistake? Did they hear God or not? Because they persisted in trusting God, He blessed them by performing miracle after miracle for them.

When Carlotta Barfield felt God was calling her to leave her comfortable life in Florida to begin a ministry in Georgia, she too had a lot of reasons to wonder if she had heard God's voice—but He gave her His miraculous direction every step of the way.

THE VOICE THROUGH THE WILDERNESS

October 1994
Southern Florida
As a single mother with three dependent children, this was not a convenient moment for Carlotta Barfield to make a major career move. However, she strongly suspected that God was calling her to do just that. It would be such a significant change, and the logistics of obeying this call left her in such a state of uncertainty, that she decided to fast for forty days just to make sure she was correctly understanding how God was leading.

Said Carlotta: "For two months, the Lord kept encouraging me to prepare myself for ministry through encouragement from others. And I was hearing God's urging in my spirit, too."

As practiced by Jesus, His disciples, John the Baptist,

Daniel, and others in the Bible, Carlotta fasted by limiting her nourishment for a prescribed time period. She fasted by eating only one meal a day for forty days and by eating nothing for seven days and nights. During this time, Carlotta said that she kept to herself and fixed her mind on the Lord. To seek God's face, she prayed at noon and midnight.

"I had a midnight prayer line going," said Carlotta. "A bunch of us would get on the phone at midnight and pray for direction for my life and other things. I had a lot of godly women agreeing in prayer with me."

During her forty-day fast, God spoke to her powerfully. "I believed He was urging me to move back to Georgia," said Carlotta. Because the Bible instructs believers that God's direction will be "established by the testimony of two or three witnesses" (2 Cor. 13:1 NIV), Carlotta received confirmation of her leading from God when a brother in Christ called her from Atlanta with a similar word of advice.

Perhaps God sent these strong messages to Carlotta because, like Abraham, He was asking her to take her children and launch away from job security and safety into the unknown. Said Carlotta: "On my job, I had just been promoted to the Critical Care Unit, and I was making more money than I ever made. I was living in this townhouse I was renting from a woman in New York. She said I could buy it. I was in a good financial position and there was no reason why the loan shouldn't go through, but I prayed about it. The Lord impressed on me, *I told you to move to Atlanta!*"

But Carlotta still hesitated, this time for another, more personal reason. Carlotta and her husband were separated. "He was a believer when we married, but he backslid and left me with three kids. I was still hoping for reconciliation. I was thinking about him all the time instead of what God wanted. At times like that, you need other believers around to encourage you."

Finally, however, she told God, "Okay, Lord, I'm going, if You want me to go. I'm taking my children, my clothes, the TV and VCR—and that's it."

When Carlotta arrived in Georgia, things went smoothly for only a very short time. She and her three children moved in with her sister and brother-in-law and their four children. He was the pastor of a church, and he was anticipating Carlotta's help. However, trouble soon erupted.

"The enemy—I mean Satan—rose up," said Carlotta. "My sister and brother-in-law said our kids didn't get along, so they put me out."

Carlotta then stayed with her mother, who was not a Christian believer, but that, too, was troublesome. "Nothing that I did was right in my mother's eyes," recalled Carlotta. "At the same time, I was unable to find a job for a month."

Carlotta applied at various hospitals, but each time, the door shut in her face. Finally, as she was driving through the tiny village of Alma, she saw a sign pointing to a hospital. She was surprised a town that small had a health-care facility, but she felt that God was urging her to follow the signs. She did and applied for a job.

The assistant director of nurses hired Carlotta on the spot. She started to tell Carlotta that her beginning wages would be $12.00 an hour, but the director of nursing broke in and offered her $8.50.

"I was going to get up and leave, but I felt the Lord was saying, *Stay here*," said Carlotta. So she accepted the job.

There were still conflicts between her and her mother, but Carlotta said that God comforted her by impressing on her that He wanted her to live near her mother. "There was nothing around where my mother lived, so I thought maybe I should buy an old house and move it by her," said Carlotta, but somehow, she knew that wasn't right either.

Because she had encountered so many problems since her move, Carlotta began to seek God's face for guidance. Again, she went on a forty-day fast. "Why did You send me down here, Lord?" she asked.

About that time, a friend from Miami called Carlotta to encourage her. "When the Lord sends you places, you're going to go through a lot of bruising and bumps," she told Carlotta. "God lets these things happen to test our faith, to see if we are really going to stick to what He has told us—no matter what."

Once Carlotta realized that her problems in Georgia were not shut doors but tests of her resolve to be obedient to God, miracles began to happen in rapid succession. First came peace on the home situation. With the aid of some $1,000 in gift certificates, Carlotta was able to purchase a new, doublewide house trailer, even though she was only making a paltry wage. Her mother invited Carlotta to place the trailer right beside her home, sparing her from having to purchase or rent land. Then her sister and brother-in-law apologized for making her leave their home. They asked her to work with them in their church, but Carlotta felt that was not what God wanted her to do.

Instead, she applied for and received licensing in a reputable church fellowship and began another midnight prayer line. Shortly thereafter, Carlotta heard that a new radio station had opened in a local town. She felt that God was leading her to begin a broadcast of encouragement to believers on this station—but it was such a leap of faith that Carlotta held back.

"In December of 1998, I was convinced that God wanted me to broadcast," said Carlotta. "I need the money to do this," she argued with God. But as the months passed, God's Spirit persisted in encouraging her to begin a broadcast. In January, God seemed to say, *Go to the radio station.* In February, she felt the Holy Spirit urge, *Go to the radio station.* In March, again God seemed to say, *Go to the radio station.* Finally, in April, she realized she needed to stop talking about getting on the radio and just do it. *Take your tithe and buy the time,* the Spirit whispered.

Carlotta did, buying fifteen- and twenty-minute spots.

Three weeks later, a man came into the radio station asking to see Carlotta. He had heard Carlotta on the radio and came to pray with her to commit his life to God. Shortly after, he began to financially support the radio ministry.

Since that time, the radio ministry has developed into a church also. When Carlotta looks back from where she began and to where she has come, she says she is amazed at what God has done to bring her this far. "The Lord sure is keeping me," said Carlotta.

Carlotta Barfield and her three children live near Atlanta in Paxlet, Georgia.

*S*aul of Tarsus was a classically trained Jewish theologian with a mission: He planned to purge the civilized world of the teachings of Jesus Christ. He was enjoying considerable success at it, too. Legal documents in hand, he prosecuted Christian believers everywhere, putting them to death and seizing their assets.

On his way to Damascus to stamp out an enclave of Christendom, however, a light came from heaven and the voice of Christ told Saul that he was on the wrong side of the issue. The voice changed Saul forever (Acts 9:1–19).

Al Kasha, a famous composer and writer, was in a prison of his own making. Then he saw the Light of Christ and heard His voice, both in a figurative and literal sense.

THE MORNING AFTER

1978

During the days that should have been the happiest of his life, composer and writer Al Kasha's soul lost harmony with his life. Nagging echoes from his past drowned the present moment's applause. Yesterday's ghost voices shouted today's compositions in discordant off-key.

Al had chosen a tough industry, show business, in which to make his mark. Yet his career was solid gold. He had already won two Academy Awards for compositions hummed by nearly everyone in the civilized world (the theme from *The Poseidon Adventure*, "There's Got to Be a Morning After" and the theme from *The Towering Inferno*, "We May Never Love Like This Again"). He had a loving wife and a beautiful daughter.

But Al's early life of struggle and strife in Brooklyn,

New York, still haunted him. His father, a violent alcoholic, had delivered daily beatings to Al's mother, brother, and Al, leaving emotional scars that were slow to heal. His mother, lost in her own twisted world of mental illness, played sadistic mind games with her children, pitting Al and his brother against one another. Years later, with talent and perseverance, Al had escaped the torture chamber that was his home, only to find he had constructed a jail within his own mind: Al had agoraphobia, the fear of leaving his house.

"I was a prisoner in my own home," said Al, "and it was threatening to ruin my personal life. I took heavy doses of prescription drugs to keep me relaxed. They helped a little but not a great deal."

Al happened to see a television show, "60 Minutes," in which agoraphobia was mentioned. The show reported that a doctor in Menlo, California, had experienced some success in treating this debilitating disorder. Al immediately called the doctor, who requested that Al come for a consultation.

"How am I going to visit you if I can't leave my house?" Al asked him.

The doctor told him about a support group for agoraphobia, but Al could not parole himself from his self-inflicted house arrest to attend those either. However, the support group sent someone to try to desensitize Al to the terror he felt when passing over his doorstep.

"They helped to a point," said Al, "but I was still in my in-house prison. I was praying for help even though I wasn't a believer."

Because of Al's fears, his family life was approaching ruin. "My wife and I were having problems. When you are agoraphobic, you don't want your family to leave the house because of the danger you see out there—so you have a phobic family, too. I was also frightened to be alone."

Al and his wife, Ceil, finally separated. Living in a friend's apartment, Al was close to suicide.

Sunday, October 8, 1978
3 A.M.
Now apart from Ceil for three weeks, Al was in despair over his life. Everyone he loved was out of his reach as surely as if he was locked in a dungeon. Not only was he estranged from his wife, but although he had visitation rights with his daughter, he was too chained by fear to leave the apartment to see her.

In the early morning hours, Al tuned the television to a Christian broadcasting station. As a Jew, he was praying for God's help—but it came in the form of a gospel sermon.

The preacher spoke on the text of 1 John 4: 18–19: Perfect love casts out fear. Said Al: "The writer in me transposed the words to 'Fear casts out love.'" Al was living the truth of that. His fears had indeed cast away the loves of his life.

"I put my hand on the TV, and in front of God, I asked for His help," said Al. "Suddenly, a tremendous heat enveloped me, and the whole building shook. Although I was in an apartment with all the windows shut, they opened, and a blinding light poured in. I felt the face of God and I heard Him say, 'I love you and you are My son.' That's all I wanted to hear my whole life."

The fear instilled by a violently abusive father and the rejection of a mentally unstable mother flooded back, only to be met and extinguished by the healing tide of God's love. "I felt a powerful pressure in my chest. I could barely breathe," said Al.

What happened was beyond Al's comprehension, but he knew this: God loved Al Kasha perfectly. His love cast out Al's fears.

Later that morning, Al had his once-a-week opportunity to visit his daughter. Although he previously had been unable to visit her because of his agoraphobia, today would be different. "I got into the car and I thought, *God's perfect love casts out all fear*," said Al. He drove to his former home and rang the doorbell. Ceil was surprised to see him on the doorstep, but an even greater shock was awaiting her.

Pat, a Christian friend and a former student of Al's, was also visiting the home at that moment. She was taking Ceil to church and she extended the invitation to Al, also. "Al, would you like to go to church with me this morning?"

To Ceil's great surprise, Al agreed. "What are you going to church for?" his wife asked him. "I converted to Judaism from Catholicism for you!"

Nevertheless, the entire family went, driving over the California freeways that had previously terrified Al to a church in the San Fernando Valley. Al and Ceil were barely speaking to each other, so they seated themselves on opposite ends of the pew, with Pat and their daughter, Dana, between them.

The sermon was on Song of Solomon, John 3, and John 4. When an invitation was extended to accept Christ as Lord, Al said, "I walked down one aisle, and Ceil walked down the other aisle." Not until later in the day did they each discover what the other had done. Their commitment to Christ led them to recommit themselves to each other.

Their newfound spiritual adventure was just beginning. A young man named Clark left two Bibles in their house. These Bibles were written in easier-to-understand translations, and Al and Ceil began to study and learn.

Two weeks later, Clark knocked on their door again. "I lost my job. Can I move in with you?" he asked.

Ceil was a little dazed by all the sudden changes. "First we are Christians, now we have people moving in with us!" she said.

"It turned out to be a real blessing," said Al, because in the eleven months and two weeks Clark stayed with them, he took Al and Ceil through the Bible from Genesis to Revelation.

Al and Ceil also joined a Bible study, but four months later, the leader had to drop out. Al and Ceil asked one another, "Why don't we take over the Bible study?"

They did, and it grew to between eight hundred and one thousand people. With cars choking the neighborhood and limousines pulling up to leave off attendees, the police soon came knocking to see what was happening.

Before God delivered Al from agoraphobia, he couldn't live up to his success. "It was part of being a perfectionist," said Al. "Enough was never enough."

The perfect love of God cast out that fear, too.

Al Kasha has continued to make his mark in the world of entertainment as a songwriter and composer. He writes songs and musicals encompassing both Christian and secular themes, such as China Cry *and the score for* Seven Brides for Seven Brothers. *He has also written several books, including a pamphlet on agoraphobia entitled* "Faith Over Fear". *The Bible study assumed by Al*

and Ceil has grown into a church known as Oasis Christian Fellowship. Al's deliverance from agoraphobia is complete. He comfortably travels around the world to teach songwriting and ministers at universities. Al, Ceil, and their daughter Dana still reside in southern California.

*I*n the midst of a catastrophic drought in the land, ravens fed Elijah. No food was to be had anywhere for any price, but morning and night, the birds brought him bread and meat (1 Kings 17:1–6). This was extremely odd behavior for ravens, for they are scavengers and notoriously greedy. Food was just as hard for them to come by as it was for everyone else in the land of Israel. However, at God's command, they carried enough to feed a grown man. On yet another occasion, God sent food to Elijah via an angel (1 Kings 19:5–7).

When food was scarce for a missionary's family in war-ravaged Bangladesh, God sent them food via angel express, while protecting it from plunderers along the way.

POSTMARK: HEAVEN

Bogra, Bangladesh
February 1974

Even in the best of times, hunger was an ever-present specter in Bangladesh. One of the two poorest countries in the world during the mid-1970s, it waged a war of independence with Pakistan and, with the help of India, won. But even though the fighting was over, the country was still flooded with starving refugees.

Not long before, food aid had been shipped into Bangladesh's southern harbor of Chittigong. Armed guards were placed around the supplies to keep malnourished people from stealing it. But while the fledgling government tried to wrangle a way to distribute it, the food rotted on the docks. People were starving everywhere.

Into this situation Dr. Victor "Vic" Binkley brought

his wife and four young children from Indiana to Bogra to set up a new surgical unit at the Christian Hospital. Although the kids were very small, the gravity of the situation was not lost on them. Said Vic's eldest daughter, Laurel: "Fifteen or twenty beggars would come on Sunday morning, little children with swollen bellies and hungry people. We'd give them coins and rice. When we went out of the compound, we'd see terribly skinny people and you knew they were sick."

The family was moved into the second floor of a mission house on a compound, where they lived with other missionaries and about two hundred hospital employees. A single woman who was a longtime missionary shared her Bengali cook with the family, and they took their Spartan meals together.

They ate local vegetables, such as lentils, coconuts, cucumbers, and jackfruit. (Known as "poor people's food," jackfruit is a close relative of the breadfruit. A large fruit as big as a basketball, or sometimes twice as big as a basketball, it grows on the trunk of a tree. The "green" taste is described as something like a chestnut; the ripe flavor is said to be sickeningly sweet.) A small quantity of whole wheat flour was occasionally available from the government. Generally, this was made into "hot rudies" by combining the flour with water, rolling the paste into balls, flattening them, and frying them on an inverted wok. Rice, the staple of the local people, was in short supply.

Vic and his family had been in Bangladesh only a short time, and although they had brought food items with them, they were down to their last four or five cans of beans. The food boxes packed by stateside churches would not begin arriving for several months.

All of the people on the compound were eating the same limited local foods, and when a food box arrived for one of them, they shared the goodies with Vic's children, ages one to six. But the food boxes that arrived were always opened, half of the contents missing or stolen.

The monotonous diet began to be a constant topic of conversation among the children. They knew food was hard to come by and that it simply couldn't be purchased at the corner. Said Laurel, "I remember hearing there were only a couple cans of beans left, and we children thought we'd help out. We got down on our knees and prayed for a food box. We just assumed it would come today. We were determined that it would come today."

"Now don't expect too much," the children were cautioned by others who knew how impossible it was for food to arrive within such a short period. The adults were also concerned that the children would be disappointed if food didn't arrive immediately. "It takes three or four months to get a food box from the United States," they told the kids.

The children, however, were undeterred. They believed the food would arrive yet that day. They continued playing, and they were not surprised when a Jeep pulled up at about three o'clock in the afternoon.

"Mom! Mom! The food box is here," they called.

The box weighed about thirty pounds and was about fourteen inches square—and to everyone's surprise, it was unopened. Inside was their favorite pizza mix, macaroni and cheese, and wonder of wonders, chewing gum.

As Vic examined the box, he was in for another surprise: The box had been sent from the United States only the week before. The sender had posted it for surface mail, which usually cost about $30. However, somehow the box was sent airmail, a very expensive process.

Or perhaps it came via angel mail.

"The box was intact, the contents fresh, and exactly what we needed. I was pretty delighted to see it," said Vic. "Everybody was surprised but the kids. They were expecting it."

Dr. Victor Binkley and his family served for nine months in Bangladesh. He has been a surgeon for thirty years, having spent the last ten on various mission fields, primarily Haiti. Dr. Binkley has six grandchildren. Laurel Binkley Gorney is a homemaker with two preschool children and lives in Fisher, Indiana.

Conclusion

Someone asked me recently if all answers to prayers could be classified as miracles. My reply: "I think it's a miracle that God even listens to our prayers, let alone answers them!" And it truly is.

All over the world today, millions of people will ask God for divine intervention in their lives. Some will request healing for a sick loved one, safe travel for a child returning to college, a job, financial assistance. . . and the list will go on and on to even include the vague "Bless Grandma and Grandpa" prayers. The astonishing fact is that no matter how many requests are laid before the throne on any given day, God will decide how best to answer those prayers according to His sovereign plan, while taking into consideration the needs of the individual. He doesn't simply initial our request memos in a spare eternal moment sandwiched between reading the fallen-sparrow reports and the hair-number inventory sheets. He gives each request His full attention as if He had only this one request to answer and only this one soul to love. So when God answers a prayer, yes, I think it is a miracle.

Occasionally, though, He puts a flourish or two on a prayer request, makes a bit of a production out of answering one—and people immediately classify it as a "miracle." Sometimes people are so completely amazed that God bothered to answer a prayer for them that they forget to be thankful for the answer itself! And that, too, is a miracle: that God answers the prayers of we sinful people.

But what is even more surprising is that He invites us to come boldly before His throne so we can make our requests and obtain His mercy. Even with all of the requests He receives, He still wants to hear from us—you and me—because of His everlasting, tender love for us.

Now there's a miracle!